MW00967347

Gal's Guide Anthology

Women of History

Edited by Lindsey Taylor of Four-Eyed Media

Gal's Guide Press
Noblesville, Indiana

Gal's Guide Anthology: Women of History

Copyright © 2022 by Gal's Guide to the Galaxy and Gal's Guide Press
All rights reserved, including the right to reproduce this book, or portions thereof, in any form. Authors retain the rights to their own work. All works are used with permission.

Gal's Guide Library
First Women's History Lending Library in the United States
107 S. 8th Street
Noblesville, IN 46060

www.galsguide.org

ISBN 978-0-9898132-3-5 paperback

First Edition: March 2022

Cover design by Leah Leach
Interior artwork by Leah Leach

For the gals
who guide us

Table of Contents

Introduction

The birth of a first daughter awakened a mother bear in me. I didn't know a person could 100% unconditionally love another person so much and yet be so protective at the same time. I vowed that I would fight for her dreams to become a reality and that I would protect her from as many nay-sayers as I could. The problem was I didn't know how to do that.

At the time of her birth, I wasn't going after my goals anymore. I was settling in the title of army-wife - and now - new mother. Nothing much was expected of me from others, but inside, I was disappointed. I wasn't doing the things I said I would do - the things I wanted to do.

Hours after a new human passed through my body, I sat there in the military hospital, and I became determined that this new little life needed someone who didn't just say, "go out there and live your dreams;" she needed someone who would show her the successes, failures, and hard work along the way. I needed to be the example. I need her to see that I worked hard for my dreams whether they were easy or hard. I needed her to see that success doesn't come to you - you go after it.

I wanted to go into the ring of life and get knocked down and have her see me get back up again. It was the only way I knew how to really show her how mean this world is and how worthwhile it is to stand up for the things you believe in.

I didn't have female role models growing up. I had a few teachers, but there was a wall up that separated that connection between teacher and student beyond grades and attendance. Most likely because of that Police song "Don't stand so close to me..." Instead, I watched a lot of movies and imprinted onto male characters for ways to live a human life. The male guise, the male point of view, is what I saw.

But when I started seeking out female role models and then later women of history, I saw a new perspective. There were stories I had never heard before. There were stories of not trying to be #1 but instead trying to do something better for the greater benefit of the community. I saw women who were the smartest in the room but not listened to only because of gender identity.

Learning their stories, seeing them overcome obstacles that were FAR less complicated and problematic than my life, I started to feel less isolated. I started to feel less pinned down and more connected to this wide spectrum of sisterhood. I started to feel those gals built a pretty solid foundation. What if their stories were a blueprint? What if, when we connect to women of history, we connected to the mother bear in all of us?

When Lindsey Taylor of Four-Eyed Media came to Gal's Guide with the idea of an anthology in May 2020, I loved the opportunity to have a variety of voices talk about women of history. We had also at that time recieved a grant from the Pacers Foundation to host a writing workshop. The idea of having students in the writing workshop work on a piece to submit to the anthology would be a wonderful opportunity. Writing is harder when you don't know the audience or if it will see the light of day. Then again, once a writing piece is done, the idea of the audience reading it can be scary as well. So I guess it's fair to say all writing is scary - unless you're in a writing class with me.

For 12 weeks, I hosted the Gal's Guide: Mother of All Memoirs Writing Workshop. We went through topics like: why write about women, why write about women's history, what is Hero's Journey by Joseph Campbell, and how is it different from Heroine's Journey by Maureen Murdock? We did writing exercises that pushed us to see how vital our voices were and how needed they were in our community. I didn't push the writers hard; I simply believed in them. I tried to guide them to their own inner voice and amplify it back to them.

Every single writer in the class brought something different to the page. Not all of the students in the class are in this anthology, but many of them are. I'm proud of each and every one of them for showing up but mostly for putting aside their inner critic and telling their own story. A writer isn't creative; what a writer is, is brave.

We all learn something new every day whether we like it or not. Women tend to learn more things and go inward. Men tend to learn more things and go outward. What if we did both? What if we took the time to go inward and sucked up knowledge, lessons, and stories like the bellows? What if, when we were ready to take this knowledge into the world to help others, we exhaled like those same bellows? What if we did this many times over in our lives?

Inhale - Learn. Exhale - Share.

Maybe the world could breathe together again.

Maybe I'm wishful-drinking.

What I do know is that I now have two wonderful daughters who call me "momma bear" and a few writers who call me "momma writer." I'm the luckiest gal in the galaxy.

Dr. Leah Leach
Noblesville
February 2022

"The future isn't just a
place you'll go.
It's a place
you will invent."
- Nancy Duarte

Beginning

By Lisa Meece

Lisa Meece designs learning for corporations and people, whether in her corporate job as Learning Manager or in her volunteer role for Starbase Indy. She also works to help people connect with themselves and others through her work with Holding Space, LLC.

There were heroes, once.
Shattering glass ceilings, slaying dragons with the shards.
Toppling towers of absolute authority
With power the powers disbelieved.
Walls at borders never breached
Crumbled as they roared.

We believed them, once.
Believing each victory was final, fair, and full.
Raised on tales of total triumph.
We embarked, confidently secure
History had promised us
We could have it all.

Disillusioned, now
Struggling with the skeletons of dragons once thought slain.
We build on the shifting sands of unclear expectations.

Bound to fail, unless we understand
This work is never finished,
It can only be begun.

*"I always thought of my
mother as a warrior woman,
and I became interested in
pursuing stories of women
who invent lives
in order to survive."
- Lynn Nottage*

"I'm not afraid of storms,
for I'm learning how
to sail my own ship."
- Louisa May Alcott

Mothers at a Science Fair

By Dr. Leah Leach

 Dr. Leah Leach is the founder of Gal's Guide to the Galaxy. Because of Leah's deep dive into women's history, she has developed a new writing method for educators and writers. The Born of Many Mothers Method (B.O.M.M.) combines women's history and mythology with a focus on empathy.

My work with Gal's Guide Library combined with my filmmaking and mythic storytelling background has developed this visual exercise. Designed for healing, creating, and empowerment, this story is something you can add to and reconnect to when you are feeling as though you are alone in the galaxy.

The women you meet in this exercise were real women of history; their words in this story are taken from quotes that have been said.

A visual exercise.

Find a cozy place to sit. Take a deep breath. Relax your limbs. Activate your visual imagination.

Imagine walking up a paved driveway in the countryside.

The dawn is casting a magic yellowish glow on the deep green trees in full bloom. Each tree catches the light in different ways in between its leaves and pine needles. Behind the trees, you see there is some kind of structure; you know it will reveal itself soon. Until then you enjoy the gentle walk in nature.

Safe in the nests of the trees, you can see and hear mother birds feeding their hatchlings. Ground animals are on the hunt for food.

Around the bend, the trees give way to an immense castle. Turrets and roof peaks seem to touch the clouds. Countless and immense windows arched with craftsman details. The castle sits on the hillside as if nature has left a spot specifically for the foundation of this beautiful building. The expanse of the castle grounds can be seen from left to right, but it feels as though it's bigger than the eye can take in.

As you approach the castle, the energy welcomes you. The closer you get to the castle the more you can see - people in the windows waving to you, and they can't wait to see you.

The driveway leads you around a circle to the front door. Between the circular driveway and the front door, there is an area of stone pebbles and pavers. The pavers are engraved with one word on each.

You

Belong

As you stand on each paver, you feel a whirlwind of healing energy.

The door opens and the butler, Eldridge Oswin, greets you welcome. Eldridge has a kind face and a quiet persona. He's the type of man who would tell you when you have something in your teeth but do so in a way where you feel loved and not even attempt any shame spiral.

"Welcome," says Eldridge. "We are delighted you are here; we have been waiting for your arrival with great excitement. Please explore the castle and its grounds. Everyone here strives to help you."

The foyer of the home is bathed in light from vast windows on multiple floors. The checkerboard tiles in the foyer create an inviting path to the center of the castle. Women stand in front of tables with either chalkboards or tri-folded boards that have their name and what they should be most known for.

Reminiscent of a school science fair in the gym (but far more elegant), all the women of history have gathered to help you learn how to find happiness, heal, and spread compassion into the world.

Gertrude Jekyll (1843-1932) adds sweet peas and chrysanthemums to an ornate vase at the front of the room. The light fragrance of the flowers is soothing. Gertrude is a stocky English lady with fresh flowers in her wide-brimmed hat. Eldridge softly approaches you, "We are fortunate to have Ms. Gertrude Jekyll here today. She created over 400 gardens in the United Kingdom and America; between writing and breeding new plants, she is a busy woman."

Just then there is a sound hammering. "Ah, Ms. Marie Curie," Eldridge says as his head motions across the room.

Marie Curie (1867-1934) stands behind her table in the foyer hammering rocks and then holding them up to the light to see if the rocks contain any uranium. Her well-worn navy blue dress has rock dust on it, and her left pocket seems to be glowing from the radium she keeps with her. Her grey hair is piled atop her head in a messy bun. It's hard to tell if her hair is grey because of age or stress. Marie notices you and says, "I was taught that the way of progress was neither swift nor easy."

You approach Marie's table, and she tells you about her life in Poland, how both her sister and her mother died before Marie had her tenth birthday. She left her homeland for Paris to study chemistry and was introduced to Pierre Curie by a fellow physicist. Their work in the lab brought them closer, but Marie first said no to his proposal of marriage.

"Pierre Curie came to see me and showed a simple and sincere sympathy with my student life," Marie says. "Soon he caught the habit of speaking to me of his dream of an existence consecrated entirely to scientific research, and he asked me to share that life."

Marie tells you how she wanted to move back to Poland. She tries to control her disappointment in the fact that her homeland wouldn't allow her to continue her education and research because of her gender. Choosing a scientific life with a partner, Marie and Pierre married in a non-religious service in France; the bride wore navy blue. Two years later, the couple's daughter, Iréne, was born.

Marie says, "In 1903, I finished my doctor's thesis and obtained the degree. At the end of the same year, the Nobel Prize was awarded jointly to Becquerel, my husband, and me for the discovery of radioactivity and new radioactive elements."

Marie would be the first woman to win a Nobel Prize in any category. She would win again five years later, and this time Pierre was not with her. Pierre would die in a tragic accident on the streets of Paris. When crossing the Rue Dauphine in the rain, he tripped and fell under a horse-drawn cart, killing him instantly.

Marie dedicated herself to her work, founding two centers of medical research and helping with x-ray technology during World War II.

"Nothing in life is to be feared," says Marie. "It is only to be understood. Now is the time to understand more, so that we may fear less."

You thank Marie for her knowledge and take your leave.

An elegant Japanese woman dressed in a purple kimono walks past you carrying a stack of books. One falls, and you pick it up. The cover reads The Tale of Genji. You offer to help with the stack of books. She leads you to a bookcase in the great foyer where she introduces herself as Murasaki Shikibu (973-1031), the author of the world's first printed novel.

As you place the classic books on the shelf, she tells you that Japanese women of her time were not allowed to learn the Chinese language, even though it was the language of the government. Murasaki was not the first of her family in the literary arts; her grandfather and great-grandfather were well-known poets. Murasaki's father was a scholar of Chinese classics and was given a governorship.

"When my brother....was a young boy learning the Chinese classics, I was in the habit of listening to him, and I became unusually proficient at understanding those passages that he found too difficult to understand and memorize. Father, a most learned man, was always regretting the fact: 'Just my luck,' he would say, 'What a pity she was not born a man!'"

Murasaki doesn't mention her mother, as it is possible she died in childbirth. You allow her this privacy as shares her story.

Murasaki would not marry when it was custom. She would stay close to her father until her late twenties and travel with him on business. She did, however, marry a much older and wealthy government man. Even though the two would have a daughter, the marriage lasted about three years because her husband died in the Cholera epidemic of 1001.

"I felt depressed and confused," Murasaki says. "For some years I had existed from day to day in listless fashion ... doing little more than registering the passage of time ... The thought of my continuing loneliness was quite unbearable."

She began writing in a diary, publishing poetry, and writing a fictional account of the courts, you know, the world's first printed novel.

With each publication, there were people upset with her writing in a language reserved for men. Murasaki turns to you and says, "I am wrapped up in the study of ancient stories ... living all the time in a poetical world of my own scarcely realizing the existence of other people ... But when they get to know me, they find to their extreme surprise that I am kind and gentle."

You agree that Murasaki is kind and gentle as you hand her the final book for the shelf. She bows to you and heads off to collect more books.

You notice a grand staircase with women traveling up and down. Some in a hurry, some having idol conversations on the stairs. One woman is carrying a model of a volcano that is about to erupt. She shouts to make room as she giggles and says, "Why are these always here?!"

Eldrige approaches and extends his arm and motions his hand to the other side of the foyer. "Why not start in room number one?"

You nod and approach the threshold. Atop the door, there is a tiled mosaic that reads, *Empathy Room*.

This meditation is one you come back to time and again. You can create the rooms of the castle to be the things you want to learn and the women who have given you lessons along the way. They can be real and imagined. When you complete your time at the castle, Elridge hands you a note that lets you know that the castle and all its grounds have been gifted to you. All the women inside would like to stay and help you. There is room for more guests, and rooms that have yet to be explored.

I call this the Born of Many Mothers Method. It's a book I'm working on that gives you more examples of women in various rooms, but for now, you get to fill the castle.

If you are stuck in your life, I hope that you'll return to the image of the castle and walk around until you find the answers you are looking for. Connect with the mother energy that is all around us- it's here to guide us.

*"I was taught that the
way of progress
was neither swift
nor easy."
- Marie Curie*

*"A woman with a voice
is by definition
a strong woman.
But the search to find that voice
can be remarkably difficult."
- Melinda Gates*

For the Tomboy Who Liked to Call Herself Jimmy

By Mark Andrew Heathcote

Mark Andrew Heathcote is adult learning difficulties support worker. His poetry has been published in journals, magazines, and anthologies. From Manchester, he resides in the UK. Mark is the author of *In Perpetuity* and *Back on Earth* published by a CTU publishing group, Creative Talents Unleashed.

Katharine Hepburn at her chiseled youthful best
Frankly-wasn't she eye-catching in a peculiar way?
Her eyes, their gaze unashamedly transfixed me.
It was a spell just anticipating where next
They would jolt and come to rest. To me-
She seemed otherworldly, like a cannonball that's
About to be fired - not in anger or destruction.
Simply as to astonish and reawaken dulled senses,
Simply as to jettison through the stratosphere,
Show anyone of us can fly and be immortally idolized.

Hepburn was a force of nature, a precious talent.
She was like a bushfire burning out of pure devilment.
Or smiling with satisfaction a tempestuous hurricane
That would righteously carve its-own unique path.

Hepburn was a woman I came to greatly-admire.
She was to epitomize the 20th-century "modern woman"
In the United States, but she was more than that?
She was the assertive woman, a torchbearer for the future.
She was indeed headstrong, spirited, and, yet, grounded.
And yet thought while taking her daily ice baths,
"The bitterer the medicine, the better it was for you."

Pivotal Pages

By Patricia Rossi

 Patricia Rossi is writer and freelance artist. Her written works have been featured in literary journals, newspapers, and magazines. She facilitates writing-to-heal workshops for cancer survivors, a writing/book club for severely disabled adults and has created female-empowered writing workshops.

It happened more than fifty years ago. Father Time's pendulum has rhythmically clanged and swung, days have tumbled into decades, but nevertheless, my recollection is indelibly etched. I close my eyes, concentrate; I am there once more.

It's a Saturday afternoon in late October. I'm a senior in high school, searching the card catalog's alphabetized drawers as amber hues of sunlight filter through the library's window. I spend almost every Saturday at the library browsing through tightly-packed aisles of fiction and non-fiction books, reading poetry, delving into history articles, perusing newspapers, magazines and squinting feverishly in fascination as I comb through historical microfiche. My social studies textbook has designated an entire chapter to westward expansion, describing in elaborate detail the life and times of the early pioneer, his exciting expeditions to vast and uncharted territories, his imminent discoveries far and wide.

Admittedly each time I push open the library's entrance door and settle in at one of the large mahogany tables, often desecrated with a classmate's carved initials, I too feel like a pioneer; albeit my exploration is purely intellectual. I'm not crossing barren land, trudging through fields, scaling treacherous terrain, but I too am searching, looking for answers, grappling with the possibility of stepping beyond the only boundaries I know. I burst with awe and appreciation as to the plethora of opportunities available at the library to learn, discover, and awaken my soul. Every crevice of its brick and mortar is richly layered in thought-provoking concepts to embrace, ways to continually challenge me, engage in analytical thinking, leisurely reading, academic fact-finding, pursuing artistic ventures, learning a new language, paging through astronomy books, traveling the solar system, or blasting off to Mars via a science fiction novel.

I revel in dizzy merriment at the library's endless options; however, my weekly visits to the library serve another purpose. It provides a sense of solace and comfort as I wrestle with a major decision tethered firmly to a looming deadline. I am anxious and confused about my future. I wholeheartedly adhere to and relish the library's strictly enforced "quiet" requirement. I much prefer the soft and hushed whispering on a Saturday afternoon at the library to the boisterous hoots and hollering of my high school's home football games attended by practically the entire town. Traditionally, the victorious home games are followed by a parade of honking cars driven by screaming, rambunctious classmates. The parade invariably ends in the local diner's parking lot as teenage revelers tumble out of their cars and spend the rest of the evening carousing along Main Street.

For me, Saturday afternoons at the library always end in the same manner. I am absorbed in a book or an interesting article only to be interrupted by a sudden booming voice emanating from a static-wrought loudspeaker announcing the official closing of the library in exactly fifteen minutes. I am prompted to hastily gather books to check out. However, it's the Saturday in late October that ends quite differently; it proves to be life-changing. Most evenings, especially in the Fall, it's sunset when the library doors lock, and I begin to walk home. Quite often the surrounding neighborhood is dramatically wrapped in a crushed tangerine velvet as the sun begins its' glorious descent.

The church steeple is cast in glistening shades of gold. At the post office, the American flag waves majestically beneath skies sketched in fire hearth embers. So too, the storefronts on Main street, ablaze in a rich autumn palette. I yearn to write a poem that captures this picturesque landscape. I wonder just how Emily Dickinson would describe the very same sunset my eyes are blessed to behold. I am certain her words would waltz across the page. I ponder about Georgia O'Keeffe's depiction; I envision her vibrant sweeping brush strokes.

I continually dream about taking a poetry, art, or writing class. But where? Such courses are unheard of at my high school. The curriculum offered is proudly declared as "practical" by the administration and PTA. Female seniors, like myself, are required to enroll and successfully complete Home Economics, a readiness class that teaches students how to properly set a table, cook, sew, and iron garments with intricate pleats. As the females are mastering domestic skills, the male seniors are required to throw on a tool belt, try out woodworking and basic carpentry, and if that proves to be futile, the suggested alternative is to pop open a car hood and consider auto mechanics as a career.

Invariably on my evening walks home from the library, I carry a toppling stack of books precariously nestled in my left arm. Fellow classmates driving their father's Oldsmobile or their revved-up Chevy Novas notice me and beep incessantly. Their sudden greetings are never a friendly gesture but rather a malicious attempt to alarm me. Without fail, it works every time; I am startled and proceed to drop my unwieldy pile. As I quickly gather my reading materials now strewn about the sidewalk, my already ill-feeling is further exacerbated. I am an outcast, an academic misfit.

I perpetually wear a coat woven in threads of awkwardness and shyness, patterned no doubt in wallflowers. On Monday mornings, conversations float through the hallways and homerooms detailing highlights from the weekend, dates, parties, and who is confirmed as going steady. My fellow female classmates brandish their gold-plated promise rings and flaunt necklaces dangling with inscribed heart pendants. I, too, don a necklace, an albatross, embellished with strands of uncertainty and fear tightly clasped to an imminent personal decision as time-frames and cut-off dates quickly approach. Constant chatter about wedding ceremonies immediately following our high school graduation; pending marriage proposals and honeymoon destinations echo through the school cafeteria and gymnasium. I dismiss it, and in its place, I deliberate over pursuing further education, college, possibly attending law school. Whenever I verbalize these potential aspirations, brows furrow, heads are scratched, and the prospect is questioned and proclaimed completely unnecessary and absurd.

Frequently the giggling babble about married life centers around the boy next door or, even better, a handsome young military man in his neatly-pressed uniform, perfectly fitted white cap, and polished shoes, deemed suave and romantic. But what did I and the other seniors really know about military life? In hindsight, we knew absolutely nothing. Our textbooks, class lectures were silent, intentionally void as to meaningful discussions of the raging war, protests, racial injustices, and women's rights.

The clock is ticking, time marches on, and I continue to struggle with making some sort of determination with respect to what to do with my life after high school. Certainly I could, akin to the other girls, find a local job, perhaps the ever-so-popular mother's helper, an apprentice-type position. If that proved unsuccessful, the town bakery or the fabric shop. Once simple employment was secured, I could then wait patiently for Prince Charming to wander down the street, approach my parents' door and ask me to marry him, and we would live happily ever after. I seriously consider the scenario but remain baffled, full of angst. I have questions. Who is he? Where is he? More importantly – should I be waiting?

And then it happened............

On that Saturday afternoon in late October. It was right after the booming announcement warning all library patrons to check out their books as the library would be closing in fifteen minutes. I head down an aisle with my stack of books, make a quick left turn in an attempt to be first in line at the check-out desk, and suddenly I see it - it immediately catches my eye. A lone hardcover book on a cart waiting to be properly re-shelved. It is bound in a bold red book jacket, white capital lettering grace its cover with the title, *The Feminine Mystique*. The title alone intrigues me. What is this book possibly about? Who wrote it? I begin to quickly page through the book; the author's words immediately resonate with me. I grab the book from the cart and gingerly balance it on the very top of my pile.

I race home and voraciously read chapter after chapter. My thoughts are validated by the author. A female should pursue education beyond high school; it's not preposterous, but rather it is practical, responsible, and quite logical. I am moved by the passages in the book. I find them influential and insightful. The author's message soothes my soul, is a catapulting force, providing the exact dose of much-needed inertia. My apprehension dissipates; I realize that I can and should reach beyond the traditional role relegated to the female. And so... I do. I remove the old Underwood typewriter from the closet, dust it off, insert a new black ribbon and carbon paper. I begin to type college applications, double and triple checkboxes as my heart races. And now... more than half a century later, prominently displayed atop my bookshelf, a first edition of *The Feminine Mystique*. Directly above it, my college diploma, framed, and next to it, my law school diploma.

Thank you, Ms. Betty Friedan, for inspiring me to "be the change."

*"We must tell girls
their voices
are important."
- Malala Yousafzai*

Herstory

By Theodore Perkins

Theodore Perkins is a fifteen-year old non-binary person. A student at Carmel High School, Theodore hopes to one day be a professional writer. They are very close with their older sister, Natalie, who inspires them to try their hardest and persevere when the going gets tough.

How many greats
Have been lost to time,
Buried under
Lesson after lesson of a
Male-oriented history class
In a male-oriented world

The French fighter,
A warrior woman
Brandishing a sword
Striking her opponents down
Proving that men are not as tough
As they like to think they are

A fiery lass
Sailing the high seas
In search of treasure?
Perilous journey?

31

Planting seeds of
Adventure in my heart and
Determination in my mind

My too-many-greats grandmother
Chipping away the patriarchy
While it was still being built
Laying foundations
We still build on today

They steal a part of her
To experiment and learn from
Still using it today
To help others survive
But nothing can cover
for the injustice of nonconsent

My mother, sister, best friends, and more
They'll pave new paths
And I'll be right there next to them
Where I will gladly join
In the breaking of the
Glass ceiling

When I Taught Women's History

By Lauren Coodley

Lauren Coodley began her career tutoring students and teaching psychology at night school. In 1996, she received a second M.A. from Sonoma State University. Her books include: *If Not to History: Recovering the Stories of Women in Napa,* and *The Land of Orange Groves and Jails: Upton Sinclair's California.*

The women in history I admire are the women who created women's history.

I never planned to teach history, never planned to be a teacher, never heard of something called women's history. I had no plans; I was a girl who grew up in the Fifties, who left home in the Sixties, and who identified with many in my own generation resisting the Vietnam War, not planning a career. But by 1976, I was teaching at Napa junior college, where a counselor who ran the new Women's Re-Entry program suggested I create a class about women's history.

My only relevant experience in the topic was from 1972, when I participated in a play called, "Susan Elizabeth and Ernestine," about three 19th century suffragists, written by Elise Wakerman, and performed by my women's group in San Francisco. I played Ernestine Rose, a flamboyant Pole whom 99% of American women have still never heard about. In 1973, I helped create a film with fellow students in a Comparative Literature class about women writers. In the script, we quoted from *Sisterhood is Powerful*: "Whatever happened to our history?"

In 1963, Gerda Lerner had created the first women's history class, while still an undergraduate at the New School for Social Research. Lerner, whose biography I would write for an *Encyclopedia of Historians and Historical Writers,* taught first at Sarah Lawrence College where she established the nation's first master's degree program in women's history and at the University of Wisconsin-Madison where she launched the first Ph.D. program in women's history.

I take down from my shelf those dusty yellowed paperbacks that I turned to in the beginning. The key theoretical assist: Sheila Rowbotham's *Hidden from History,* the pioneering collection of short biographies; Eve Merriam's *Growing Up Female in America: Ten Lives*; June Sochen's *Herstory.* I've since learned that all three of these women, plus Gerda Lerner, were also leftists. These women had come of age during the war against the Nazis or the Red Scare. They'd participated in anti-Vietnam protests. Their search for important women, like all of ours, was subjective and based on their lived experiences and beliefs.

With these slim tools, at 26 years old, with no background in history let alone women's history, I began to teach. Because my students weren't used to reading for pleasure, it was important to me to share the classics that proletarian writer Tillie Olsen had rediscovered: *The Yellow Wallpaper*, by Charlotte Perkins Gilman (whose utopian fiction we would discover later*); Life in the Iron Mills* by Rebecca Harding Davis (whose son is still famous for his portraits of early California, his mother forgotten); Agnes Smedley's *Daughter of Earth*. The Feminist Press republished most of these. *Kindred* by Octavia Butler, we only had in xeroxed form. We read *Sister of the Road*, a memoir of a woman hobo, as well as the letters of Calamity Jane, printed by Shameless Hussy Press, run by a woman who called herself Alta.

Students would read these gorgeous testimonials, write about the connection to their own lives, and share in small groups. In many ways, classes resembled the consciousness-raising group I'd been part of in early 70's San Francisco, the group that produced the play we performed. I always read their writings and commented on responses like these that follow.

Andrea wrote:
Mary Wollstonecraft and her husband lived across the street from each other. Victoria Woodhull believed in free love. All these women are inspirations because they show the messiness of life the way it truly is. These women show and prove by their lives that I can be me, live as I really am, and be a success. They also prove to be wise warnings that sometimes there may be a price for a full-throttle fight for the things you want.

From time to time, we would perform some plays ourselves, using "readers theatre" where the students were given scripts the very day of the reading. We had mock debates and did role-playing. Students researched and wrote about their mother or grandmother's lives, an end-of-class project that replaced exams and morphed into creating children's books in homage to a female forebear.

Susan wrote:
I still can't believe that Elizabeth Cady Stanton was not mentioned to me in all my years of school. I am 28 years old and I am sorry to say that I voted for the first time ever this year. I never realized the power I have as a voter and now that I have learned what it took to gain the right to vote I will never take my privilege for granted again.

In the beginning, the classes were small, 15 or 20 students. It was an elective, and no one knew what to expect. Every year, I asked the students to list the women from history that they knew. After 35 years of teaching, the lists never varied: Rosa Parks or Harriet

Tubman, Marilyn Monroe or Madonna, Hillary Clinton or Geraldine Ferraro. No suffragists, labor activists, early women scientists, inventors, or artists.

Lisa wrote:

My new list would look like this: Elizabeth Cady Stanton, Mary Wollstonecraft, Susan B. Anthony, Lucretia Mott, Sojourner Truth, The Grimke Sisters, Elizabeth Smith Miller (Bloomers). I have learned of so many great women in our history I never knew before,... I try to teach my female friends of these great women in history.

One semester, I taught a class at the local school for pregnant teens. *Ms. Magazine* had published stories of women during the Revolution when they posted warnings about bad men on trees. The teenagers wrote their own versions of such warnings about the men they knew. Incendiary and cathartic to then read them aloud!

Jamie wrote:

All these women were strong-willed and devoted to what they stand for. Like me I will not stand by and let people take advantage of others. I want to make a change in the world. I want to make it better for people that are less fortunate than me. These women should have been my role models instead of great men of the world I want my children to have women and men equally as their role models. So when I do have children be it boys or girls I will make sure that they know everything I didn't as a child.

I wanted to recognize the crafts that women like my grandmother had created. I gave students the option to create quilts, embroidery, clothing, and recipes to honor the past. Seeing the young men proudly displaying their quilts is a memory I'll never forget. By the end of my career, there were 3 classes of 50 students every semester, and the class met the U.S. history requirement for graduation. After I retired, the requirement was removed, and the class is now taught only at night by an adjunct instructor, a reflection of the backlash to much of what the women's movement had achieved.

Sandra wrote:
This is the story of my life and the struggle of a world that was ignorant of my needs, and of young women in general. I have learned so much through your class about the struggles women face on every level. I have begun to see my worth as a human being and as a woman. I have been equipped with the knowledge that we all face undeniable injustices and hardships as women.

The women I most admire created the discipline of women's history out of nothing: Linda Gordon wrote a transformational essay entitled "Towards a Radical Women's History." Sheila Rowbotham's philosophy on the history of the "common woman" along with Judy Grahn's poems about this "common woman" was powerfully influential. Foundational texts included films like Dorothy Fadiman's unknown history of reproductive rights, Connie Field's *Life and Times of Rosie the Riveter*, and Lyn Goldfarb's *With Babies and Banners*, about the Women's Emergency Brigade in Flint organizing auto plants; these were my sword and shield. My students wrote letters to the women in the films and to the authors of the books they read.

Neil wrote:
Being a man, I am thankful to have attended this class... I feel that I now have a new closeness with women that most men do not possess. There is a bond I have formed with the opposite sex that cannot be broken. If there were in the times we studied I believe I would have been right there beside some of the great women. Trying my best to fight for the better of humanity and mankind.

In teaching "women's history," I realized there was a powerful history of both women and men struggling to improve conditions in America and in the world. I became a teacher of American, California, and even Napa history, finding and placing in those fields many of the inspirational figures that most of us have never heard about. I wrote a biography of male feminist Upton Sinclair. The way I taught women's history, as the pioneers of the field had created it, was consciously a working-class and multicultural story about women's lives and the social movements that brought changes in America.

In My Humble Opinion, She Outshines Every Star

By Mark Andrew Heathcote

Mark Andrew Heathcote is adult learning difficulties support worker. His poetry has been published in journals, magazines, and anthologies. From Manchester, he resides in the UK. Mark is the author of In Perpetuity and Back on Earth published by a CTU publishing group, Creative Talents Unleashed.

My first real boyhood hero was Barbra Streisand;
honestly, I couldn't have been more than 7 years old.
I guess it's an odd choice for a boy of that silly age.
I first recollect seeing her in black and white
when a movie she starred in was first televised.

I watched cross-legged completely-transfixed.
I was in absolute awe of her charm, beauty, and wit.
I was falling in love with her vivaciousness, her energy;
the movie was about some troubled young woman
who was visiting a psychotherapist to quit smoking?

The film was made in 1970 and was aptly called
On A Clear Day, You Can See Forever.
I say aptly because as she undergoes hypnosis,

she sees herself reliving a tragic Victorian romance.
It's a past life, and something I felt then a connection with.

Most childhood heroes go on to disappoint;
they somehow wain and become less current.
But Barbra has too many strings to her bow
and never disappoints. I've noticed how oddly irritated
others view such people with abundant talents.

"Her introduction to me that day was a revelation."
All that followed was also "reverently admired."
She was the first-ever woman to receive
the Golden Globe Award for Best Director,
an award no other woman achieved for some 37 years.

And that voice who seriously has matched it since?
In my humble opinion, none have come close
as any heroes of outstanding talent - therefore go?
Streisand ranked the greatest female Billboard artist of-
all-time, and not just pretty and quirky, she's my superstar.

The Roar Heard 'Round the World

By Trudy Krisher

Trudy Krisher is an award-winning author of eight books. You can learn more about her at www.trudykrisher.com

"And then the most astonishing thing happened: The crowd began to roar. The roaring came in a rolling wave, gathering at the far edges of the crowd and then sweeping to the front. It was a tsunami gathering force deep in the ocean of history and then plunging across the world, its beaches, its cities, its farmlands, its mountains, sweeping the entire globe. It felt like church. Like something sacred, transcendent, holy. Decades of silence had been given a voice." – from *On The March: Novel of the Women's March on Washington* written by Trudy Krisher.

I could never have written those words – or understood their power – until after I had participated in the 2017 Women's March on Washington. It was an event that deepened my understanding, expanded my creativity, and changed my life. Women are said to be shy about revealing their age: not me! I was proud to have hauled my

70-year-old self onto a bus outside a Wal-Mart in Dayton, Ohio, on January 20, 2017, for the 17-hour round trip to Washington, D.C. I was proudly wearing a sturdy pair of sneakers (my knees!) and silently wearing a pair of Depends (my bladder!), thankful for the balmy winter weather that didn't require a heavy coat (my shoulders!). Throughout the experience, I heard hundreds of women cheer, shout, and exclaim: "I've Never Done Anything Like This Before!" #MeToo!

But I almost didn't go.

I'd never walked a picket line, stood on a corner waving a sign, or protested on behalf of anything before! That doesn't mean I didn't share deep sympathies with those who did. But I was a writer, one of those creatives whose noisemakers were the clickety-clacks and tappity-taps on the keyboard of a computer. The writer in me had always been an observer, seldom a participant. It was in my nature to notice, to perceive, to witness. After all, those observations gave me the novels I had published. Social justice themes were peeking out from under all their covers – I had just never held up a banner on a street corner before.

As a result, I was an unlikely participant in the Women's March on Washington. But then my minister-friend, the late Reverend Gregory Martin, encouraged the women of his congregation to march. He held a prayer meeting for us in the days after the election, a healing spiritual exercise in acknowledging our disappointment. I had come to know Reverend Greg as we worked on a team to create worship services, so he knew that I had been an active leader in the local campaign to elect Hillary Clinton. He knew how important it was to me to elevate a qualified and proven *woman* candidate into the Presidency for the very first time. He knew I was heartsick: at 70, I would likely die before I'd see a woman elected President of the United States.

So, like thousands of other women who were also heartsick, I decided to march.

Like those other heartsick women, the march transformed me. After January 21, 2017, other women ran for office, launched non-profits, and raised their voices like never before. I decided to write a new novel. After all, my motto (and likely yours) is #shepersisted.

On The March: Novel of the Women's March on Washington became a work of historical fiction. In it, the lives of three women collide when they travel by bus together in 2017 to the National Women's March on Washington.

##

Henrietta Oldham is an elderly woman who runs a failing antique store.

Birdie Jackson is a shy African-American teenager who is marching at the insistence of her feminist aunt.

Emily Messer is a recent college graduate who needs more in her life than her job as a barista and the love of her dog.

Although Henrietta, Birdie, and Emily appear to have little in common as they begin their ride from Kansas to Washington, D.C., they find common bonds in shared experiences of sexual harassment, pay inequity, self-sabotage, even bra-stuffing. As the women begin to know and trust each other, they each start to discover their voice and cultivate the courage to share their secrets.

Echoes of my own experience "on the march" are woven through the book. Like Birdie, Henrietta, and Emily, we acknowledged our fears that there might be violence or that we might be arrested. Like Birdie, Henrietta, and Emily, we crowded the trains, bumping elbows with tuxedoed Inauguration-goers from the night before pressed shoulder-to-shoulder with thousands of marchers in pink pussy hats. Like Birdie, Henrietta, and Emily, we carried signs: FREE MELANIA; IF YOU'RE NOT OUTRAGED, YOU'RE NOT PAYING ATTENTION; THERE WILL BE HELL TOUPEE.

Like Birdie, Henrietta, and Emily, we met women we might never have met before: fictional Babs Mildenhaus who was meeting a group of women soccer players from Afghanistan and who passed out buttons saying "Equality is a Team Sport"; fictional Amanda Raymond, a prosthetist who created artificial limbs for wounded vets and then had to fend off their sexual advances; fictional Belinda Gaspard, a high school English Teacher of the Year who had to give up her job to a man who didn't know the difference between "your" and "you're," but who could coach the high school basketball team.

Like Birdie, Henrietta, and Emily, we learned about advocacy groups we'd never heard of before: Women in Islam, National Domestic Workers Alliance, State Administrators of Vocational Rehabilitation, National Resources Defense Council, The Family Caregiver Alliance. Women swarmed the streets and avenues of Washington, D.C., marching for a fifteen-dollar minimum wage, for health care initiatives for sex workers, and for the ethical treatment of animals. Like Birdie, Henrietta, and Emily, we encountered life lessons that we could take into our hearts and into our communities when we went back home. "Asking doesn't work"; "Tears are the liquid form of anger"; There are three stages in a woman's life: "Pampers, Kotex, and Depends." Like Birdie, Henrietta, and Emily, we found ourselves in the presence of feminist leaders: Gloria Steinem in her red fringed scarf; Gwen Carr in her leopard print belt and "I Can't Breathe" sweatshirt; above all, Ashley Judd, decked in suffragette white and pearls, riveting the crowd as she launched into her dramatic reading of the "Nasty Woman" poem.

And after that, the roar: *"The roaring came in a rolling wave, gathering at the far edges of the crowd and then sweeping to the front. It was a tsunami gathering force deep in the ocean of history and then plunging across the world, its beaches, its cities, its farmlands, its mountains, sweeping the entire globe. It felt like church. Like something sacred, transcendent, holy. Decades of silence had been given a voice."*

And I had been, too.

"*Freedom is never really won.*
You earn it in every generation."
- Coretta Scott King

*"It's not the load that
breaks you down,
it's the way you carry it."
-Lena Horne*

When You're the Strong One

By Lisa Driscoll

Lisa Driscoll has been writing short stories since she was twelve. She vowed to dedicate her future to writing and has since put other stories into the universe. She has published in *Harness Magazine*, *Havok Season 2*, and is working on a novel. She lives in Florida with her family and a chocolate lab named Sequoia.

When you're the strong one no one calls to check on you.
No one knows the breadth of your suffering.

You take on the problems of others, but no one can see how much the pain bears down on you.
No one can see the weight of their problems on top of yours, pulling you down into the cesspool.

You hold your head up high and tread water, but under the surface, you're kicking, and kicking...
You feel yourself start to sink, but you never let that smile crack.
Because you tried that once and it scared people away to see your true darkness.

So, you claw your way through, alone.
You fight, you scratch, and your silent screams go unheard.

You make it out alive, but just barely, a changed person.
Now you face the world a different person. You're confident,
cocky even. Until someone new comes along...

At first, you try to tell yourself that you've got enough for the
both of you, but it's never enough.
You'll give it to them because you still crave that human
connection, and then you feel yourself sinking again.

But you'll survive because you're the strong one.

Limber As a Rag

By Angie Klink

Angie Klink is the author of ten books. She has written blogs for *Ms. Magazine* and the American Writers Museum. Klink has received sixty-one American Advertising Federation ADDY Awards. She also received an Honorable Mention in the Erma Bombeck Writing Competition. www.angieklink.com

"My Wonderful Life"

My son, Jack, had to make a timeline of his life for school. It was 2003, and he was instructed to mark each of his twelve years with a significant event. I dug in the attic for his baby book, and we sat together at the kitchen counter, paper and color markers before us. He was exuberant, thinking of all of the events of his short life as he drew a line across his paper, his hand rising into the air with youthful fanfare. He knew his life was happy, so what was there to fear?

I relished thumbing through Jack's baby book and reminiscing, reading his milestones aloud. On his timeline, Jack marked the year he lost his first tooth, scratched through chickenpox, started kindergarten, took piano lessons, and graduated from elementary school.

So many wonderful memories of being a young mother and raising Jack swirled amid this project. I recalled the joy of playing tooth fairy for the first time and helping him create a self-portrait sidewalk chalk drawing that included those pesky chickenpox. I remembered his first-day-of-kindergarten photo—his white-blonde hair and sweet, anticipatory smile.

At his timeline's 1998 mark, Jack proudly wrote that his brother Ross was born. For 2001, he drew an airplane hovering next to the Twin Towers.

Jack's life rolled out before us in bright blue, red, yellow, and purple markers. The squeak and the chemical smell of the felt tips filled the kitchen. At the top of his paper in bold cobalt, he wrote with a flourish, "My Wonderful Life!"

And I thought, *Yes, his life is wonderful.* It warmed my heart to know Jack recognized and appreciated that his life was magnificent.

Then I worried.

I worried for those children who had to complete this assignment and record their not-so-wonderful lives. Some students' timelines might include the death of a parent, an illness, a divorce, or some other tragedy. By the grace of God, Jack's timeline was filled with goodness all of his days.

As he bounced in his chair with anticipation to tell the world about his momentous existence, I continued to feel a gnawing unease.

I glanced down at his timeline.

Silhouettes of Jack's grandmother and great-grandmother floated onto his paper. They were figments, of course, that only I could see.

In my mind's eye, our foremothers nudged me to think about their lives, casting a pallor over my good time, unbeknownst to Jack.

I had been interviewing my 85-year-old mother, recording an oral history of her life. The conversations we had been sharing about her past began to float in my head and then settle around my heart like a treacherous fog.

I saw the juxtaposition of Jack's life with that of my mother's. Her childhood, she admitted, was not a happy one.

Chapter 1 The Orphanage

The raven-haired little girl sobbed in a crib. At age five she was too old for a baby bed. But the matron at the Crawford Baptist Industrial School for Orphans placed her there, imprisoned for convenience, while the older children attended the worship service in the next room.

She wanted to be with her big sister, to seek comfort from her substitute mother, but at ten years old, Ruth was at the church service with the older "orphans." The upright piano plunked away, and through her soft cries, she heard the distant voices of the children singing the hymn *In the Garden.* Each word pulled more tears from her hazel eyes and onto the starched crib sheet that countless other children had slept and wept upon since the opening of the orphanage in the early 1900s.

The little girl was Rosemary Lawhead, my mother. And the orphanage ensnared her earliest memory.

"I was small enough that I had to go to the nursery." Mother recalled decades later. She looked away as if seeing the memory out there in the ether, far away.

"I remember lying in a baby bed and crying. And I'd hear them having church, and they'd sing that *In the Garden.* And to this day, I can't stand that song."

She shook her head slightly with disgust. Or was it disbelief?

I come to the garden alone, while the dew is still on the roses.

Alone, she was, but far from any garden paradise. And she was a Rose, but far from the hope that the morning dew brings.

Rosemary sobbed in an orphan's bed, but she was not an orphan. Her parents Ross Vest Lawhead and Della Dove Lawhead were out there beyond her garden of loneliness.

The church service tore my mother from the only security she knew at the orphanage—her big sister. "I just clung to Ruth's dress tail all the time. I was scared, you know. She was like a mother to me. I slept with her. As far as I was concerned, Ruth was my mother."

On a spring day perfumed with thawing earth, my grandfather took my mother and her three older siblings to the orphanage in a horse and buggy, clip-clopping past 30-miles of cattle and cornfields. It was 1923. Charles was 12 and Ruth was 10. Louise, 7, lived part-time at the orphanage and part-time with a family named Locke. "I guess they liked her," Mother speculated. The baby of the family, two-year-old Ross whom the family called "Junior," stayed with family friends. Brother Carl would be born in December of that year.

My grandfather and his children traveled from their home in Frankfort, Indiana, to what an advertising brochure described as "The Crawford Baptist Industrial School, a home for helpless, homeless children of Baptist parentage of Indiana. Situated on 185 acres of land two miles south of Zionsville, Indiana."

...and the voice I hear, falling on my ear, the Son of God discloses. And he walks with me, and he talks with me, and he tells me I am his own ...

As my mother cried in the crib, she learned the meaning of the word "orphan." It meant your parents leave you. It meant your sisters and brothers go away. It meant you are no one's *own.*

Before they left Frankfort for the orphanage, someone took a picture of my mother with her siblings and father. I first saw this photo when I was a young mother in my thirties and my son Jack was a toddler.

My Uncle Carl brought the black and white photo to my mother when we gathered one day at my house. He looked pleased that he had unearthed the photo from some dark closet and made a copy to present. When the photo was taken, he had not yet been born.

Mother stared at the 80-year-old image and said, "I think that is right before our Dad took us to the orphanage."

I looked at my mother. "What?"

Did she say <u>orphanage</u>?

Mother chuckled softly and continued to stare at the snapshot, fingering it a little too much, her thumb moving up and down at the corner. *Always handle photos on the edge,* I thought. *So as not to damage the image*.

"Angie doesn't know about that," my mother said, presumably to my Uncle Carl, but perhaps more to herself.

"We were in an orphanage for a little while when Mom was sick."

I felt dizzy. A little out-of-body. Thoughts ricocheted through my head. *My mother was in an orphanage. But she had parents. How on earth did that happen? And furthermore, she had kept her orphanage stay a secret for my entire life.*

I looked at the 5 by 7. It was the first time I had seen a photo of my grandfather or an image of my mother as a little girl. I examined her innocent face. In the snapshot, Mother's head is slightly bowed as her eyes gaze sheepishly up toward the person with the camera. Her wavy dark hair is cut short. I could see my adult mother in that tiny, vulnerable form. Her outer self. And her interior.

My mother had always been a quiet, sometimes sad person who loved her children. She was overprotective. Fearful of what could happen to me. Fearful of life.

In my shock, I stammered a few questions, but Mother's answers were vague as to why she went to an orphanage when both of her parents were very much alive.

"It was just for a few months," she said.

So much to unpack. I needed time to think. Jack was running around the room holding up his latest Lego creation. Subconsciously, I thought I would learn more when the time was right when we were alone. The matter was dropped for cheerier subjects, and we headed out for lunch at a restaurant. Because she knew I was intrigued with the old image and lived in a circa 1900 home where I liked to display vintage black and white snapshots, Mother said she would leave the photo with me for safekeeping.

I also believed that she left the photo with me so she did not have it as a reminder of what she chose to forget.

Later, I placed it with other family photos I displayed on an antique table in my living room. From then on when I walked nearby and happened to glance at the photo, I thought of *orphanage,* and a shadow fell over my mood.

About ten years later, I began to interview my mother about her past. My freelance writing career was advancing. The bits and pieces I knew of my mother's rather tragic life sounded like a book to me. In fact, I often thought that if all of my mother's sorrows were written into a novel, readers would think it was over the top. Too much. Get real. How could one person endure that many misfortunes? It would be unbelievable for a fictional character to experience all that befell my mother. Sadly, my mother's heart-rending stories were very much real. Yet I didn't know many details, as I was her late-in-life baby she brought home from the hospital on her forty-first birthday.

So, I began to interview her before it was too late, and she was not with me anymore. Mother was agreeable because it meant we spent time together, one-on-one, as she was lonely in her assisted living apartment. I also think she was flattered that I wanted to learn more about her life. My curiosity validated her feelings and experiences, although I did not consciously recognize that then. Perhaps for the first time in her life, she could tell her side with no sibling, parent, or husband present to question, judge, correct, smooth over, spin in a different light or deny.

During one of our interview sessions, I handed her the pre-orphanage picture and asked her to tell me about it.

"Frankly," she said. "I think that was taken just before we went to that orphan's home." She remembered the moment of time the picture captured and the layers of sorrow therein, yet she acted as if this was her first realization that the picture was taken hours before she was labeled "orphan."

Upon hearing her words, I felt somber helplessness.

"Now I don't know how this all happened. My dad did all the arrangements."

She hesitated and continued to gaze at the snapshot I had placed in a vintage gold frame. Perhaps seeing the photo elevated to "frame-worthy" bolstered my mother as she told her difficult story. The frame said, "Hard times are important to acknowledge."

In the photo, my mother, her siblings, and father sit staggered in height, tall to small, on a ramshackle wood step. Their shoulders overlap, almost enmeshed as if melting into each other would keep them safe, and the bleak journey before them would not happen.

Ross does not look at the camera. He gazes into the distance toward his children, yet not directly at them. Who held the camera and snapped the trigger? Who does Ross Lawhead not look in the eye?

Ross is thin and handsome in his tie and cap. He works as a fireman and extra engineer on the Nickel Plate Railroad between Frankfort and Delphos, Ohio, where my mother was born. The chain of his pocket watch dangles from his vest pocket. Vest is his middle name for it was the maiden name of his mother, my great grandmother, Amelia Annie Vest Lawhead. She died when Ross was 12. Leaving him "half an orphan" to be raised by his father.

Is he thinking of the orphanage where he will soon take his children? Is he admitting to himself how his selfish actions brought his family to this hopeless point? Is he remembering the pain of losing his own mother at such a tender age, the same age as his eldest child, Charles?

All of Ross's children look at the camera. They are dressed in their Sunday best. Charles sits next to his father. The pain of the impending separation is evident on his 12-year-old face. He is old enough to understand. How much does he know? Like his father, he is dressed in a white shirt and dark tie. His hands are folded, fingers interlaced and resting on his knees, mirroring the pose of his father.

Next to Charles, Ruth, in her dark dress with a wide, white collar, eyeglasses, and unruly hair, is smiling with her arm around my mother. She is her protector. My mother wears a dark dress, high button shoes, and thick black stockings. She looks *not unhappy.* Perhaps watchful. Innocent. Unaware.

As I looked at the photo, my heart ached for this little girl who grew up to become my mother. She trusted the adults who were her caregivers. At least at this point. Before everything changed. Before her father rode away from the orphanage, alone.

Thoughts flashed in my mind. *I am related to these children who sit on a rickety wood porch and would soon experience the type of pain that I, thankfully, never knew.* The thought was hard to hold.

... and the joy we share, as we tarry there, none other has ever known.

" I think we were at the orphan's home six months," Mother said, still holding the photo. "I can't remember too much about Charles being there."

An article in July 4, 1906, *Baptist Observer* gives a description of the offerings of the Crawford Baptist Industrial School. Under the subtitle, "The Importance of Caring for Our Orphan Boys," it states, "It is an old saying that 'Satan finds mischief for idle hands to do,' and like most of the old adages there is a world of truth in those few words. Boys need to be employed."

The orphanage put the boys to work on the surrounding farm "until they can take care of themselves." The article also stated that the girls are easier to adopt out. Why was that? Couples didn't want boys who they assumed were more trouble? Or they want girls to do their domestic chores? Or to be the sweet and innocent child they never had?

They called the housemother, "Mom Finch." I knew this because of a memory my Aunt Louise shared. After we had been doing our interviews for about three months, Mother and I visited Aunt Louise, age 88, in her apartment. My aunt's wall-to-wall carpet was dotted with her hand-made, kaleidoscope-colored braided rugs.

Mother looked at her older sister and said, "Angie has been asking me about when we were kids. She says she is going to write a book about my life."

Mother chuckled at the novelty.

Aunt Louise sat serenely on the couch with her hands folded over her slightly rounded belly. The sofa was covered with a raucous rainbow of her crocheted afghans. It appeared that she did not consider matching colors in her decor. All shades were welcome. She liked to keep her hands busy.

Aunt Louise was a sweet, more backward version of my mother. She became pregnant at age fifteen and quit high school to marry my uncle. At the time of our visit, she had been a widow for a few years. I asked her if she remembered being in the orphanage.

"I remember one day when Ruth and I were eatin' with the other kids, and we weren't s'posed to talk, but somebody said somethin'. And Mom Finch shoved a napkin in Ruth's mouth."

The air in the tiny, crayon-box of a living room filled with the image of a napkin in ten-year-old Ruth's mouth.

I thought of my late Aunt Ruth, the oldest girl in my mother's family. I knew her as headstrong. A bit manly. She spoke her mind. She could be crass. She worried about money and paying bills but made sure she had enough to get by—no matter what it took. Once my parents went with Ruth on a bus trip to New York City. Aunt Ruth took all of the towels and toilet paper from the hotel, stuffing them in her suitcase. My father was mortified and said he would never again go on another trip with her.

For the most part, Aunt Ruth's personality was a contrast to the personality of my soft-spoken mother. Curiously, Aunt Ruth liked the song *In the Garden* and asked that it be played at her funeral. Was the song a comfort to Aunt Ruth? Did she remember it played in the orphanage? How could the song my mother detested because she associated it with her lonely orphanage stay be the hymn Aunt Ruth requested to "play her off" to heaven?

As I sat in the midst of Aunt Louise's amazing technicolor apartment, my heart sank with the sadness my mother and aunts had carried with them for their lifetimes and how their different personalities dealt with their childhood traumas.

I could see how Mom Finch would single out Aunt Ruth with her coke-bottle thick glasses and scrappy personality, whether or not she was the one who spoke in the orphanage dining hall.

After some research, I discovered that Mom Finch's name was Dora, and she was the wife of the home's superintendent, Charles Eugene Finch. I found a photo of the Finches in a write-up about the home. On a visit to interview my mother, I showed her the photo.

Mother sat in her La-Z-Boy holding the paper and staring at the image.

"How did you find this?" Mother's soft voice floated on a lilt of amazement. She appeared mystified that a pivotal piece of her five-year-old life could be held in her hand decades later.

"I contacted the Frankfort Library where they have archives of Clinton County history," I explained.

Mother continued to stare at the hazy copy of the nearly 100-year old original paper. I wondered what flashed in her mind.

With her close-set eyes and tight lips, Mom Finch stared back at my mother.

Why were the Lawhead children placed in the orphan's home? And where was their mother during this time? When I posed these questions to my mother, her memory, at first, appeared cloudy.

"I really don't know why I went there, to tell the truth about the matter," she said. "My mom and dad separated. I suppose Mom had to go to work, and they didn't know what to do with us, so they divided us up."

She paused and the clouds parted.

"From what Mom told me after I got older, I think my father had an affair with another woman."

My skin tingled, all of my nerve endings sprang into high alert as I waited for her to explain.

Again, my elderly mother told the story as if she just in that moment recalled the facts, when in reality she had kept the details inside of her for decades.

"Her name was Lena Klinger."

She knew her name!

"I remember Mom telling me about her when I was eighteen. One of the times Mom was in the hospital—this was years after the affair—this Klinger woman was working there. And she apologized to Mom. She said she was so sorry for all the trouble she had caused her."

I sat on my mother's loveseat barely breathing. My mother recalled this woman's name after all of these years? This woman had an affair with her father and devasted her life.

Mother's reveal of Ross's affair was only the tip of the iceberg of truth. I continued to interview her over the course of several months, while also talking to other family members. I was able to weave dates and events together to come up with more.

My sister speculated that Ross had women at the other end of his railroad line in Delphos, Ohio. He came home to Frankfort one day and gave my grandmother Della syphilis. Not only did Della have syphilis, but she gave birth to my Uncle Carl, and he was born with syphilis.

My mother lived at the orphanage the same year her brother Carl was born. Were my mother and her siblings "orphaned" because their mother was sick with a disease that, in the 1920s, was thought to affect only the immoral? Della had syphilis. She was pregnant, and her baby was doomed to carry the disease as well. This explains why my mother's father "handled all of the arrangements" of the orphanage and why her mother never visited the home. My hunch is that Della's father, my great-grandfather to whom she was close, took her in and cared for her while her children were given out like a litter of farm puppies.

I looked up what it was like to have syphilis in the 1920s. I read that syphilis was viewed as "a public health nightmare" and a "subject beyond the boundaries of decency." Della, my grandmother, had five children with one on the way. What humiliation and fear did she face?

I gathered my courage and decided to ask my mother about it. Eighty-one years after her orphanage stay, into my whirling cassette recorder, my mother spoke delicately of the disease that blanketed her family with shame.

"Yes, my father gave my mom syphilis. Isn't that a terrible thing to do to a woman? Then Carl was born with it. It's a terrible thing. That's why Mom was sick so much probably. That's why Carl was so sickly. Seems he was always getting sick with pneumonia or something. He was always puny. It was kind of like people getting AIDS now, but not quite that bad. But people didn't talk about it. Of course, I don't tell people about that."

And so Ross Lawhead took his children to live in an orphanage. It appears that none of his or Della's siblings stepped in to help, even though they lived nearby. Did the stigma of syphilis keep relatives from taking in the Lawhead children and giving them a temporary home? Was it the shame of their father's affair that kept the family away so as not to be associated with immoral behavior? Perhaps Della and Ross were too ashamed to ask for help. I may never know for sure.

However, I do know that as a daughter and a mom, the story of my mother's early trauma drilled a hollow in my heart that remains. My childhood and adult life are a sharp study in contrast to my mother's and grandmother's rough existences.

And my sons' days? They are golden. We walk on the shoulders of our maternal ancestors who made possible Jack's "Wonderful Life."

My wonderful life.

The difference between my sons and I is that I carry my mother's baggage of abandonment and loneliness for she raised me in the shade of her fears. Sure, my life is a success as an author, mother, and partner in a 40-plus year marriage; however, I have to continually work on living relatively angst-free, to not open Mother's suitcase of anxieties.

I endeavored to break the chain and not pass down my mother's carry-on of cares that was always stored in her overhead bin by encouraging my sons to live boldly, to become who they are meant to be without trepidation.

My grandmother Della was made a victim by her husband and the time. It was an era when women had no voice, no power, no reliable birth control, and nowhere to turn if family did not help. Two years before her husband gave her syphilis and her children went to an orphanage, she had received her right to vote when White American women garnered suffrage.

Della Lawhead's children paid the price of their father's indiscretions not only while they lived in an orphanage but for their lifetimes. The underpinning of their days endured permanent damage, and in the years to come, their individual insecurities would seep from the cracks of their personalities.

My mother remembered that her father visited the orphanage but never her mother. Perhaps, Della was too sick or too sad to see her babies and then leave them with each visit.

After six months, the Lawhead children left the orphanage and reunited with their parents. Soon after, Della gave birth to Carl. John, the seventh and final child, was born three years later, the same year a train carrying their father steamed into Frankfort, crashed, and blindsided their lives forever.

Angie Klink's dual memoir *Limber as a Rag* is the story of how she was affected by her mother's tragic life. The title comes from her mother's description of her own childhood as a self-taught acrobat. She said, "Outside, I'd do stunts, and even at the park I'd draw a crowd. Everybody would just stand around and watch me. You wouldn't think so now, but I was as limber as a rag." For years, Klink did, indeed, think her mother was as limber as a rag, an unscathed survivor of trauma. Until the accumulation of pain drove her mother to self-destruction. Shocked and heartbroken, Klink strove to save her.

Heredity and Herstory

By Barb Conlin

 Barb Conlin worked for 30+ years in Information Technology before retiring in 2020. During retirement, Barb pursued her Master's in Business Administration while beginning to nurture her love of creative writing. She currently lives in Carmel, IN with her husband Tom, and daughter, Jess.

She was a woman who suppressed her own feminine nature.
Patriarchy was the sum of masculine southern culture.

Ability to voice concerns was diminished.
Feminine woes were ignored until finished.

What didn't finish was to be managed and dealt with in quiet,
So as not to negatively alter the male climate.

Men folk thought too busy and stressed,
Dealing with everyday work, depressed.

They also could not be made uncomfortable
To deal with female cares that were so insufferable.

So her issues were to go unreported
Too long; recovery would be distorted.

She was 42 at first diagnosis
By a niece who noted the psychosis.

There were questions of how long and why,
How serious; oh, but now, how to reply?

Her illness was prolonged.
Stage three. They all felt wronged.

Followed by stage four, so vicious.
Did we believe in a God so malicious?

The news was never good, but she remained hopeful.
She retired knowing the catastrophe was woeful.

What did that mean to her life -
For her husband's sickly wife?

For her son's and daughter's mother,
For her family, friends - dare we shudder?

There would be anger and sadness and grief
Over a disease that was such a thief

Stealing time and youth and beauty and hair
And leaving everyone in such despair.

Challenges were great in their marriage;
He would forget, and she would feel disparaged.

The illness strengthened during her daughter's freshmen year,
But she knew her youngest child's success was clear.

She worried about her husband and son.
She requested her daughter be the one.

One to keep watch when she was gone,
To provide care though still to mourn.

Her daughter made her promises loudly,
And in the end, she stood proudly,

Proud to carry on with her mom's passion -
For love, care, and familial fashion.

Action to show love indefinitely,
Even when not returned commensurately.

It was never expected,
And it never unfavorably affected

The love and the care that continued.
A mother and daughter truly infused

Through genetics and history,
Hereditary and herstory.

"My story has value.
To be rendered powerless
does not destroy your humanity.
Your resilience is your humanity.
There is nothing stronger than a
woman who has rebuilt herself."
- Hannah Gadsby

Spirals

By Dr. Leah Leach

 Dr. Leah Leach is the founder of Gal's Guide to the Galaxy. Because of Leah's deep dive into women's history, she has developed a new writing method for educators and writers. The Born of Many Mothers Method (B.O.M.M.) combines women's history and mythology with a focus on empathy.

When I was in my early teens, I would find sanctuary listening to my parent's records. I loved the ritual of the process: flipping through the stacks, choosing the speed, dusting off the record with a velvet tool, laying the needle down carefully (and in the right place), and then the crackle before the music started.

I'd listen in headphones so I could hear the nuance of the music and feel surrounded by it. I also listened in headphones because I was told by my parents I was being too loud. In a room no one used, I sat in a rocking chair and stared at the books that no one read.

Music was a cocoon I could put myself in for a few minutes at a time. The world outside turned into a murmur of activity as I was surrounded by the music. I felt encapsulated, safe, snug. A bubble that kept people away and let me turn inward for a while. I could start a song or an album and felt I had achieved a metamorphosis.

I was a child of the 80's so I lived on the crossroads of records being phased out, cassette tapes being all the rage, and the introduction of CDs. I had all of them. One thing they all had in common is that they all played music using a spiral.

When you play a record, you start from the outside groove that follows along a spiral until it reaches the end at the center of the record. You can change the speed of 45, 33 1/3, or 78, but they will all follow the same spiral. If you want a specific song, the grooves are notated where the start of a song is, but it will still play in a spiral - outside to inside.

When it came to cassette tapes, the biggest plus for me was you could jump around the room, and the music wouldn't skip. There was, however, the danger of the tape getting "eaten" by the machine. I related it to ruining a record by jumping around and creating a terrible scratch. Such danger of losing the music was in both products. Cassette tapes were more portable, lighter, and I could throw them around. The best thing about cassettes was I could take them apart; I couldn't do that with a record.

The first time I took a cassette tape apart it was to fix it as the tape got twisted and rolled back onto the spool. I took the time to see all the inner workings. If a cassette was brand new, the spool on the left (supply reel) would be empty. It would catch the tape as it rolled over guide rollers in the corners that connected to the second spool (take-up reel).

Instead of a record that spiraled the music from the outside in, the cassette tape started at the inside and spooled/spiraled the tape to the outside. Still a circular motion, still not an infinite loop, there was a start and stop.

CD came in, and to my eyes gave the world a small record that could hold both sides of the music (no flipping to side B) and was not *as easy* to be in danger of losing the music. It was marketed as, "high tech," and, "the way of the future," but it was really just an evolution of what we were used to, music that plays using a spiral layout. Instead of a needle reading the information or magnetic head, it was a laser.

Once music became digital, I could download it or put it on flash drives. I could take it more places, I had it on my phone but…. I found I didn't listen to it as much. Granted I was older and life had a funny way of getting in the middle of simple pleasures, but I think the connection to the organic magic of it was gone. I missed the spiral.

Then I read Maureen Murdock's work.

Maureen was a student of Joseph Campbell.

Joseph was a famous scholar of mythology and wrote *The Hero of a Thousand Faces; he* was famous for the Hero's Journey as a way of life but also a writing tool. If you're a *Star Wars* fan, you might be aware of how George Lucas used Joseph's research to write his characters in a pattern that humans have been writing stories in for centuries.

Hero's Journey is a structure of storytelling that Joseph Campbell found through reading our myths, legends, folk tales, and origin stories. It turns out we've been telling stories the same way for thousands of years, and a pattern can be identified.

The basic pattern is that a hero is bored, they get a call to action, they find a mentor along the way, they have some trials, they meet some allies, and they battle themselves and the great powers that be. They find unconditional love from a Goddess-like spirit and return home victorious that they have gone outside themself to bring back knowledge.

When Maureen asked Joseph Campbell if women also went on the Hero's Journey, Joseph responded, "Women don't need to make the [hero's] journey, they are the place that everyone is trying to get to." Joseph thought that women were often the destination of the hero's journey, the prize at the end of the journey, the unconditional love that men need. Joseph didn't think women needed to go on the journey themselves.

Thanks?

But I still don't feel whole.

I feel like I'm on a journey of life too.

Maureen was a Jungian Psychotherapist in her own right. So she studied her patients and wrote *The Heroine's Journey: Woman's Quest for Wholeness*. In her book, she describes the journey as a spiral. You start on the outside and travel inwards toward yourself.

Hero's Journey by Joseph Campbell focuses on the first half of life for men or women. A time when you are building your identity in the world. A time when you are transitioning from adolescence to adulthood.

Heroine's Journey by Maureen Murdock takes those first steps and then asks you to do the soul-seeking work, in other words, a second quest to the center of yourself.

Full Circle

Last November, I was at Uhura Training Academy. It's a fun STEM project that Gal's Guide does to add programming to a fan-run Star Trek convention called Starbase Indy. For one of the programs, my husband, Joshua, was putting on a presentation using his record player. I joked that he would need to explain what a record player was to the crowd because it was such an *ancient* device. Turns out the room was filled with Gen X-ers and Baby Boomers so an explanation wasn't needed.

Josh was playing *Switched on Bach* by Wendy Carlos on record. I watched the record turn, and I got lost in the music. It felt different, it sounded different. I don't know if it was a physical thing to look at that I could focus differently, but I connected quicker and with more intensity.

Even though that was not a record that was on my rotation growing up, I was transported to my teenage self. I could feel the vibe of carefree adventure beneath the surface of angst, confusion, and control. That feeling that, at any moment, the ties that bound me as a child would be gone, and I could grow into my own person with my own ideas. In my teenage years, I listened to music for guidance, but I also listened to find my center.

When did I lose that?

Connecting to the music in its digital form did lose a little for my mind-body-soul transference, but also I got older too. I had kids, they had music they liked, I had a job that kept me busy, and I watched too many movies.

A few hours after listening to *Switched on Bach*, I had what the alcoholics refer to as a moment of clarity... different phases of our lives can be summed up by the metaphor of a spiral of music.

Think of an album being a different period in your life.

Adolescence as an album, each relationship has its own album, a college album, and adventures in between. Throughout a lifetime, we listen to many albums. If we're lucky, we have a variety of music to choose from.

Sometimes we listen to the same record over and over. It can be that we like that feeling, and it's a moment we want to stay with as long as we can. When I moved to the Bay area, I played The Boo Radleys' song, "There She Goes," every time I crossed the bridge to relive the scene in a Mike Myers movie that I loved. I felt that playing that song and that bridge made me feel like movies can come true.

But playing the same record over and over can also be the part of your life where you are stuck in a rut, and you feel like everything is the same day after day. Paul McCartney and John Lennon may have had that in mind in the song, "Day In The Life:" "Woke up fell out of bed. Dragged a comb across my head."

We have times in our lives when we want a drastic change of pace. In these moments, we have an opportunity to change genres. I had a 1940s swing phase that jumped to a punk phase. If I think of that 40's phase and punk phase as a metaphoric album, it encapsulates a section of my life at that moment where I learned something new. Swing music was joyful, fun, carefree, and romantic. I learned about being a partner and what I wanted in a relationship and what I didn't want in a relationship.

Punk music let me process my Gen-Xer rage with a beat that matched my own heartbeat. It was fuel to get beyond what I thought was holding me back.

There were also times when I needed to revisit past trauma. Putting on music that was the soundtrack to unbelievable pain and sorrow helped me process how far I have come. I would focus on what I had learned since the last time I was in that trauma. Revisiting it with music helped tap into that emotion and deal with what was below the surface. The trick was finding the end of the album and not staying there in a loop.

If we think of moments in our lives as albums of lessons, moods, passions, and emotions, we can start to see a pattern. We can also decide when it's time to change the music.

Spirals have a start and stop. They leave choices for you to repeat or change. They allow you to go inward to your center self, but they also let you share your center self with the outside world.

Having a favorite band, singer or song allows you the opportunity to connect with people who share your passions. It's a way of tethering your center self to the outside world. Concerts are a great experience for this. I remember once at a Sting concert, he got us all to sing the "Message in a bottle" phrase over and over until we were all in sync and in a near-trance. The power of the crowd was more moving than any record. I felt tingly and spinning. I felt I was inside and outside of myself at the same time.

Perhaps that is what a spiral means in nature, without a known consciousness, maybe by connecting to the spirals, we can learn how nature is inside and outside of us.

Tree rings grow in a spiral from inside to outside. You can fit an amplified needle into the groove of a tree ring and play it on a record player.

Galaxies are spirals that move at the same speed in the center as they do on the outside edge. Thanks to Ms. Vera Rubin for discovering this!

The Golden Spiral or the Fibonacci Spiral is worth spending a few minutes learning about. They are both above my pay grade, and I struggle at times to understand. They are a spiral that is found in the ways trees create their branches, the spacing on leaves on a stem, and even the bracts (scales) on an artichoke. The ratio of the spiral is what makes it fascinating; the mathematical calculations are found in the exact same pattern throughout much of nature.

As a kid, I would see in TV or cartoons the hypnotizing spiral. The ones that Donald Duck would get trapped into, and his big black eyes would reflect the spiral. They didn't have too much effect on me, but the idea that you could put someone in a trance from drawing a spiral is intriguing although disproved. Doctors and dentists have used them to calm patients by giving them something to focus on to take their mind off procedures, but was it the spiral that gave them comfort or just changing their focus?

The one spiral that does worry me is the shame spiral. I have gotten tangled in the vortex of this one too often. It could be something someone said or a self-criticism that echoes in my head. It seems to call up negative friends and suddenly there is a party in my head of everything negative that I've ever heard or thought about myself. Years of naming the shame spiral and choosing to stop its spin had been a lifetime of practice.

The metaphor of spirals in the record has helped. It has kept me mindful that there is a beginning and end to every spiral positive or negative. If I don't like the song, I change it. There are plenty of songs for all of us to choose from just as there are many paths of life to choose from.

I feel our purpose is for each of us to find what it means to live a human life and share that with each other. The paths are countless so if you find a path that works, share it. Even if it's as silly as a metaphor of spirals.

"Don't let anyone rob you
of your imagination, your creativity,
or your curiosity. It's your place in the
world; it's your life. Go on and do all
you can with it, and make it the life
you want to live."
- Mae Jemison

Birth of My Freshman Year

By Barb Conlin

 Barb Conlin worked for 30+ years in Information Technology before retiring in 2020. During retirement, Barb pursued her Master's in Business Administration while beginning to nurture her love of creative writing. She currently lives in Carmel, IN with her husband Tom, and daughter, Jess.

Friday the Thirteenth

I should have known better. I had seen enough of Jason and the *Friday the 13th* series at the single screen Court Theater in my hometown to know that the day was a bad omen. But on that afternoon, Friday the 13th, January 1984, I had refused to be anything but happy. Happy that I was a senior at Hamilton High and that my first semester grades were in the books. Although it had been a challenging December with 5 finals, 2 papers, and one group presentation, with Alice – whom I loathed, I had emerged victorious over the trials. I held tight to my 21st ranking in the senior class of 700+ – which ensured that my grades would support the aggressive college application process that I had undertaken during the first semester. As I learned from my counselor, colleges do not like surprises on final transcripts. I could not tell if Jackie, or Ms. Tillman as we addressed her to her face, was telling me this to scare me or not – but I was minding my p's and q's just the same.

After school, I was traveling 30 miles south to Cincinnati to visit and have dinner with my cousin, Scott, my mom's nephew, who was attending UC's Conservatory of Music. I loved Scott – he was so uniquely him and represented a different branch of our Midwest family tree. I liked his branch - Scott was very smart, reserved, and so talented with classical guitar being his forte. He was also very handsome, appearing wise beyond his years. He wore cool clothes and hats that I thought represented the worldliness of university life so well. He was also open about his sexuality - bisexual in the early 80s before I really knew what bisexuality was. He, in essence, captured what I hoped my college experience would be like - an exploration open to new thoughts, ideas, ways of life.

I was among the first to go to college on my dad's side of the family, and I could not wait to have dinner with Scott to pick his brain. I was sure we would eat at a cool Cincy restaurant that he would pick for us. Some quiet place in Clifton (if there was such a thing) or in Mt. Lookout. A place where he could sip some wine and where we could chat about his college adventures, where I could learn about all the things waiting for me as I started this journey out of high school.

So, on that Friday, as soon as the final bell terminated my computer science lab for the day, I gathered my books and happily skipped out of the classroom, spilling into the hallway with 2000 other HHS students. Lockers were flung open, weekend plans were finalized, and small groups gathered together to start their weekend. I met up with Tracy by our lockers, and we wandered down the long corridor to the exit to the student lot. Sheila waited for us at the exit, and we burst out of the doors and headed toward my bright yellow two-door Ford Escort – a little car that refused to be ignored. Bright yellow, black louvers over the window of the hatchback, and Escort scripted in black down both sides. Dad had Mr. Gilbert from across the street freehand my name in blue paint across the back. Mr. Gilbert was quite talented – he had freehanded "Motormouth" on the side of our boat – after me as I, too, could not

76

be ignored. The brisk air and threat of snow that weekend were not going to chill my spirit that afternoon – not even on Friday the 13th, January 1984.

Since my four-cylinder Escort could not be revved, we made the "vroom, vroom" sounds as we bounced out onto Eaton Avenue and maneuvered through traffic toward our destinations. Sheila was the first to be dropped off as she lived about 4 blocks away from home. Tracy and I both lived on Woodford Street. Or Woodford Avenue – depending on which corner of our one-block long road you stood on. Apparently, one of the street signs was printed incorrectly (at the time, we didn't know which one), and the city was too broke to pay for it to be reprinted. Both signs were installed as-is, and most folks adopted Street as part of our address.

The bright yellow Escort finessed down the street – which was one block long, one lane wide with street parking on both sides. Since we were home from school before most neighbors made it home from work, I easily found street parking in front of the house. Tracy jumped out and headed across the street. Her mom, Julie, was in the door waiting for her, and I gave her a holler and a wave. I loved Julie – so pretty, fun, and perpetually 28. Ish.

Our house was a white bungalow. Well, I know that is what is *now* - back then, it was just home. A small three-bedroom, one-bath house with a living room, eat-in kitchen, and a persistently wet basement. The house was built upon a little hill - a hill that was too small for sledding due to the abrupt angle between the yard and the sidewalk. The driveway proved to be better in that regard – a smoother transition. You just had to be sure to stop or jump off the sled before you landed in the road. We didn't have a garage. Few neighbors did - maybe a detached garage or a carport. We learned early about warming up the cars in the winter and cooling them down in the summer. I was lucky to have a dad and brother; Dad spoiled me or told my brother to - especially when it came to scraping off the car windows when we woke to frost or snow.

After grabbing my book bag, I headed up the uneven concrete steps and across the more uneven walkway through the yard. As I took the crumbly porch steps, I glanced up to see my dad in the doorway, ready to open up for me. His black hair was greased into place as it always was, short, almost high and tight from his Army days, and parted to the side. His ruddy complexion made him look tan all year round, and that day was no exception. He claimed Indian blood helped, but that was before DNA tests were around to confirm it. He had on his house uniform – a white t-shirt and khakis, and he was chewing on a red toothpick. Par for the course.

Although he seemed *almost* like his normal self, his expression gave me pause. He seemed flushed a bit, and his brow was furrowed. It was the look that he had when worry crept in. I had seen it before when he had to make the house payment in December or January after Christmas costs and winter utility bills were high. Or when he had to go to court to face driving under the influence charges. Or when he had to go to school because my brother was in trouble. I was familiar with the look as all of those things happened on more than one occasion.

There was no normal greeting of, "Hey, Blondie" – another nickname I picked up in addition to Motormouth. I stepped into the living room. The TV was blaring as was usual for my dad who refused to concede that he was losing his hearing. Mom could turn down her hearing aids, but my brother and I just had to deal with it.

I put my bookbag down in the recliner just steps inside the doorway and turned to look at him. If he was not going to say, I was going to ask. As it turned out, I didn't have to.

"Sit down, sis."

After I sat down, there was a long, awkward pause during which he studied his bare feet, rubbing them together as he often did and chewing his toothpick with determination. It was as if the words he needed to say were locked inside the small thin wood stick in his mouth, and he just had to get the right angle to break it open to free the words so that they could come pouring out.

It was beyond awkward.

"Dad…"

"Your mom's doctor called," he said almost apologetically. I didn't understand the tone – was he sorry for taking so long to begin to speak - or what exactly?

"Honey, it's not good."

Then, it hit me. I remembered. She had gone back to the oncologist earlier in the week after a previous OB/GYN appointment. I had been so caught up in my own excitement for the day I had forgotten that they were waiting for test results.

"So the cancer is back?" I asked pragmatically.

He nodded, and I took a moment to ponder where this was going to lead us.

"So, what's the plan? Is it another surgery, more chemo, another round of radiation, like before? Or… or what?" My questions lingered in the air like fragile bubbles waiting to pop. Or to be popped.

"It's very aggressive, honey. Stage Four. It has spread. To the lungs. He called it metastatic breast cancer. The doctor is not sure if treatment is going to work. When cancer comes back for the third time…" his voice trailed off – either in reality or in my reality.

For. The. Third. Time.

I didn't usually go to appointments with my mom, but I had gone to one back in September. We had been on our way to celebrate my birthday with dinner at Isgro's, an Italian restaurant on the East side of town. I loved that place – it was dark, and Dad let me sip his wine. I hated the wine but felt so grown up holding the glass in my hand. Sophisticated. And the Italian food was delicious. Dad said we could go to the appointment and then go to dinner. The three of us. My brother was working.

In September, the doctor had told Mom that her test results had not revealed any new growth – for which he and Mom and Dad seemed happy. He explained that if cancer came back "for the third time…" well, he didn't really explain it, but he let our emotions grab on to his words and take them where we allowed them to go. Had I not been there, I think that he would have been more pointed. Suffice it to say, that if cancer came back for the third time, it would be bad. Like crossing the streams.

I turned back to my dad. He was still talking, but I couldn't understand. Words were coming out, but it was like they were not coming anywhere close to my ears. Or maybe they were, but my ears were closed to the discussion. His words just bounced into oblivion.

Then I saw the tears, and words became unnecessary.

My dad was a man's man. He was rugged, masculine, and always right. And he was never emotional. If he was, it was because he had too much to drink. He could drink a twelve pack a night, and you would never know. If he drank too much, whatever amount that was, he would become a sappy drunk. He died in 2015, and I think that I had only seen him drunk on two occasions. And he drank daily - heavily.

Before 1984, I don't remember him crying. When I recognized what was happening, my world came crashing down. I had been attempting to wrap my mind around my mom's diagnosis logically. That was the way my mind processed information - logically. Strong in science and math and starting to dabble in programming, logic was my comfort zone. It is where everything could be assembled orderly and where everything would make sense.

My dad's crying while trying to explain to me that my mom might be dying – I couldn't process what was happening logically. My mom had suffered. For five years already. From a bitch of a disease. Diagnosed with breast cancer at 42. Facing it again, for the third time, at 47. My God. It was too much for my head to process. And my heart had no hope.

My mom and dad's relationship and life were not perfect. My dad was a good father to me, but I am not sure that I would say he was a good husband to my mom. Mom put up with quite a bit from Dad – more than I ever would tolerate. A man's man. A provider. A leader.

But there was a significant downside to that kind of bravado – at home, he was also manipulative and controlling, and he ruled the house with an iron fist - from what we had for dinner to what we watched on TV as a family to what Mom did in her free time. He made a habit of belittling both my mom and my brother, and I felt that neither thought that they were living up to his high expectations. I was the only one who came close.

From where my dad sat that day, on his spot on the couch, with, as always, an open can of Bud Light and the remote not far from his reach, his love streamed down his face in the form of salty tears. This stoic, strong man was turning into an emotional heap in front of my face. I could not process this logically.

He paused at some point – and he searched for my eyes. When I regained my focus and captured his stare, I could see and I could feel his heartbreak.

"No," I said quietly, shaking my head. "NO!" spoken with passion, a little louder.

Then, an outburst. I jumped up and ran into the hallway slamming my fists on my brother's closed doors. My tears came, too.

"Noooooo!!!!!!!!!" I screamed, collapsing in the hallway.

Dad rose and labored after me, sinking to the floor, taking me in his arms.

"We'll be ok. We'll get through this, honey. We will."

We would, but he and I both knew she wouldn't. We knew. She had let it go for too long. By the time her niece, Suzie, a nurse up in Toledo, had told her what she was experiencing was NOT normal, it was too late. She was stage three in her first occurrence. Stage three in her second occurrence. Stage four in her third occurrence – and it was aggressive. We had gone from no new growth in September to Stage Four Metastatic Breast cancer spreading to her lungs in January. It was not good.

Dad helped me up and into my room which was just another few steps away. He sat me on my bed and turned on my gigantic stereo which sat in the corner. Music distracted and then comforted me.

"Where is she?" I asked Dad softly.

"She's still at work. She will be home shortly."

"Does she know?"

"Not yet. I will tell her when she gets home."

Dad had learned Mom's fate from the doctor's call earlier in the day and shared it with me when I got home - I knew before my mom knew. I am not sure that Dad planned to tell me first - maybe he planned to wait. But after sitting with the knowledge for a few hours himself, perhaps he just couldn't contain the news. Maybe it was like a poison inside of him, and he just had to let it spew out. I didn't even try to process if it was good that I knew before she did.

I sat on my bed for about an hour and a half before I heard my mom come in. Our bungalow was so small that I could hear their conversation take place even through my closed bedroom door.

Then I heard her ask, "Is Barb home? Does she know? How did she take it?"

"Not good," was the response to the last question.

That is when I emerged from my room. Mom had moved my book bag off of the recliner and taken her seat there. She looked frail, and she looked old - especially since she was not yet even 50. The earlier bouts of chemo had robbed her of so much of her youth although her thin, straight blonde hair, lost from earlier treatments, had grown back thick, wavy, and dark. Her normal thin frame appeared fuller due to a heavy regimen of drugs over the years - including steroids. But, even with all the physical changes, she was still beautiful. I climbed into the recliner with her, and she cradled me like a baby, gently rocking back and forth with her head on my forehead.

"It will be ok, sweetie. It will be ok." She was dying yet still she was trying to comfort me. We let our tears flow and shared no other words. Again, none were necessary.

I am not sure how long we sat together, silently crying and comforting one another. Dad finally began to move around and start dinner for the two of them. I reluctantly went to freshen my make-up and fluff my hair. It was the 80s, and that last step was not only required - it was an Aqua-Net art form. I changed clothes, too. I didn't have anything that I thought was cool and hip enough for my night out with Scott; quite frankly, I didn't even have many clothes that I felt comfortable in. I picked out one of my two good pairs of jeans, Jordache, and a bright blue sweatshirt with colorful banding around the neck, sleeves, and waist. Both pieces were purchased at Florence's, the only cool clothes shop in town but one we didn't shop at often due to the higher prices. I had taken birthday money there in the fall, and these jeans and the colorful sweatshirt were the results. It would have to do.

After again fluffing the blonde locks, this time half-heartedly, I told Mom and Dad that I was taking off to visit Scott. They had, of course, forgotten. I watched their expressions to see what they thought of the idea.

"Maybe, I should call him..." I began.

"Yes, call him and let him know you are on your way. You should go, honey. It will be good for you. You've been looking forward to it." It was Mom's turn to be pragmatic. Her words resonated as final this time - we could tell. Sometimes, Dad let her have the final say. Or was it so complicated that it was the other way around? Whatever the case, Dad and I both nodded.

Dad asked if I would swing by the post office to pick up the mail before I went to Cincy. I walked to the bright yellow Ford Escort, this time with less pep in my step, and drove four blocks to the Rossville Station Post Office on Franklin Street. I opened the box, grabbing a stack full of mail. Dad was usually over every few days, but perhaps he had been distracted and forgotten it this week. I locked the box and returned to the car. I leafed through the envelopes not expecting anything for me - and then I saw it.

Miami University - Dean of the School of Applied Sciences.

I had applied in the fall to Miami University and to the Systems Analysis program that was part of the School of Applied Sciences. Jackie indicated that this was a new and highly competitive program. You could be accepted into Miami but not into the School of Applied Sciences. You could be accepted into the School of Applied Sciences but not into the Systems Analysis program. If you weren't accepted into the school or into the program but were accepted to Miami, you would start your freshman year by taking general classes and even some electives, and you could apply to the School and to the program again after semesters 1 and 2. If you didn't make it then, you would need to choose another school or major.

I was a nervous wreck. What if I didn't get in? This was THE college and program that I wanted. It was a highly sought-after and recognized program in the Midwest. And, Miami was the only school for me. Dad and I drove through Oxford, only about 20 minutes away from home, often. When we boated at Brookville Lake in Indiana, we would pass through the little town that housed Miami's main campus. Dad always marveled at the huge rotating globe that was on display in Shideler Hall on Patterson Avenue. Although you could see the globe from the road, we made frequent stops to examine it up close. It was really those experiences on campus and memories of that globe housed in the College of Arts and Sciences that led me to Miami's Junior Scholars Program with my friend, Nina.

We attended classes between our junior and senior years - lived in a dorm on campus and took classes as part of their summer session. So, although it wasn't the true college experience, more like summer camp, it made me fall in love with the school even more. I took Calculus and two Systems Analysis courses as no one advised me that taking college Calc and SAN classes in a compressed 6-week session might not be wise. As it turned out, I aced Calc even after sleeping through most of my 8 AM classes. I did well in the SAN classes, too, and I hoped all of that would assist in my application process. Both Mr. Mozingo and Mrs. King, my high school teachers representing STEM before STEM was a thing, assured me that I would do just fine.

The truth was in my hands, but I was so nervous. What if I didn't get in?

Then another question cropped up. What if I did?

Mom's cancer had just returned - apparently with a vengeance. If I was accepted and moved to campus as I had envisioned, I would not be able to help Mom and Dad at home. I could not help with her appointments which would be many. I would not be able to help with meals and house cleaning when Mom was too sick. Was that an undue burden to put on them while I was off playing house on campus? And there was the expense - both with Mom's treatments and with my college in general. It might just be too much - especially if Mom was off work for an extended time. Would Dad be able to cover the cost on one blue-collar income? Wouldn't the right thing be for me to attend classes on the Hamilton campus until we saw what developed with Mom? I could always transfer to the main campus later. Or I could commute to the Oxford campus - it was close after all. Was I being too selfish?

My tears began to flow as I sat in my bright yellow Escort, and my choices burdened me. I was in distress about what to do. And, of course, I still hadn't opened the letter. After a few minutes, the irony of the fact that my tears and haunting decisions were causing me such anguish while the letter remained unopened in my hands made me chuckle and roll my eyes. I took a deep breath and decided to open it. At least part of the puzzle would then fall into place.

Dear Miss Brockman,

After careful consideration of your application and accomplishments, Miami University is proud to notify you of your acceptance into Miami University's School of Applied Sciences...

University acceptance - check.

School of Applied Sciences - check.

I needed one more check.

In addition, you have been accepted into the Systems Analysis program for the start of your freshman year. You should be very proud of your accomplishments at Hamilton High School and here in our Junior Scholars Program. Your previous academic success is a predictor of continued success here at Miami as part of the Class of 1988.

Systems Analysis program acceptance - check!

I was indeed proud of myself. I knew that Mom and Dad would be, too. However, in the scope of the news we received earlier, was today even the right moment to share mine? What a dichotomy of a day. The dichotomy of Friday the 13th, January 1984.

Where do I go from here?

I decided to return home. Much like how Dad had probably felt earlier in the day with the bad news, I knew I couldn't contain my good news. They were surprised when I interrupted dinner. I placed the mail on the table, and I handed Dad the letter. As he read, his tears returned. He handed Mom the letter. She didn't cry but beamed with pride. She stood and hugged me tightly to her. She pulled away when she found her words.

"This is what you hoped for. This is what *we* hoped for. I am so proud of you but not at all surprised, not the least bit. You can and will do whatever you set your mind to. I will never worry about you or your future. You'll have to keep an eye out for your brother, though." She smiled and attempted a chuckle, but our joint heartbreak betrayed her light humor.

Any other day, we indeed would have laughed at her final comment. My brother, five years my elder, struggled. There were run-ins at school and with the law. There were fights with Dad. There were trouble-making friends. Stolen items. Cigarettes, pot. Bad grades. The not so unusual troubles of a teenage boy struggling to find his place in the world. Mom always teased that I would have to look after him.

However, today, regardless of her chuckle, the humor could not be found. There was such finality to her direction. It was as if she was giving me my instructions for *after* her death.

"You know, I don't have to live on campus. I could go to Peck Tech. Or even commute to Oxford..." Peck Tech was the pet name locals gave to the regional campus for Miami - located in my hometown of Hamilton. A commuter's branch.

She didn't comprehend what I was saying at first, but then realization followed by determination crossed her face.

"No. That is not what we talked about. We talked about you living on campus. And. That. Is. What. You. Are. Going. To. Do." Her words came out slowly and were pronounced with clarity and emphasis.

I opened my mouth in silent protest, and Dad shifted uncomfortably in his chair.

"Uh uh uh. No discussion this time. You wanted to live on campus. I think that it is important for you. You will learn so much more there. So that is what you are going to do. That is where you need to be." And even though she didn't initially agree to me living in Oxford, she was clear in her support that day. She had the final word once again.

We all hugged, and there were more tears - from everyone this time. They both told me that they were so very proud. And then they walked me to the door, toward my dinner date with my cousin Scott, toward my future.

I did not think that I had been in our little house, our bungalow, for very long, but it had been long enough for the snow to start. And it had not only started, but it had also come down quickly, covering the sidewalks and stealing what was left of the green from the grass. I looked up and could see the individual branches of the trees lined with the white fluffy stuff. While I loved flamboyant sprays of color offered by the fall, I loved the symbolism of the freshly fallen snow just as much. Snow in general made me feel like a little kid again - so much hope, so much possibility, such a blank slate on which my creativity could be unleashed.

Standing there, embracing my inner child, I noticed that there was a particular quiet that filled the air. Stillness. Peace and calm. I stood just below the porch taking it all in and enjoying the silence. I looked back to see Mom and Dad in the door, smiling down at me as the puffy flakes continued to fall.

I felt a newness. A birth - of sorts. I saw nods of approval as if Mom and Dad were saying - go on! Go be you. Go be uniquely you. We are with you all the way. Mom knew that is what I needed. That encouragement. That push as if to clearly proclaim that her journey was not my journey. Her journey may be coming to an end, but my journey was just beginning. She revealed to me her determination that my journey had to commence - with or without her - and that our stories, while intertwined tightly with the love between a mother and a daughter, were not one and the same.

In retrospect, I am so glad my mom had the clarity to teach me that lesson on Friday the 13th, January 1984. I loved her with all my heart, but on that day, I hated her lesson with every fiber of my being. I hated that I had to learn it. And I still do.

"I know for certain that we never lose the people we love, even to death. They continue to participate in every act, thought, and decision we make. Their love leaves an indelible imprint in our memories." ~ Leo Buscaglia, aka Dr. Love

With this quote, perhaps Dr. Love was saying that our loved ones do live forever – through those of us who survive death and continue our journeys in spite of or, perhaps because of, our pain.

I survived Friday the 13th, January 1984, as well as the Christmas break of my freshman year which included Mom's passing on Friday, December 28. The fact that I did survive surprises me to this day, but I believe that I could not have done it without the generosity of Mom's life lessons.

I was blessed to have her and learn from her for the 18 years that I did. She continued to be my guardian angel looking over me as I made my way through my remaining time at Miami, right up until I graduated on Mother's Day, 1988. During the dawning of each season of my life after graduation, I would feel newness once again and reflect on that January day. It was as if I was looking upon another pristine landscape of freshly fallen snow with Mom (and

Dad, too) behind me nodding support. Go on! Go be you. Go be uniquely you.

Forever loved, forever missed, and forever in my heart.

Rest in Peace, Mom. And thank you.

In loving memory of Dottie M. Brockman (1937-1984).

"I've been absolutely terrified
every minute of my life,
and I've never let it
keep me from doing
a single thing
I wanted to do."
- Georgia O'Keeffe

Evie's Eulogy

By Vicki Lastovich

Vicki Lastovich, the daughter of Harland and Evelyn Countryman. She is happily married to her loving husband, Mark, of 47 years. Mother of Leah Leach and Dan Lastovich. A grandma of 6 wonderful grandchildren. Vicki likes to share happiness, love, good news, good food, great times, and share great memories.

Evelyn was a beautiful Swede and a good Finlander. She had beautiful blue eyes that were filled with love. Evelyn's heart was filled with love and gratitude for her family, friends, Pastor Randy, Mount Olive Lutheran Church, Jerusha, Dr. Madhu Manoj, Allina At-Home Caregivers, and Hospice Care that helped her feel comfortable in her own home she loved so much.

Mom told me she wanted a going away party. She's going from here to heaven. This is Evie's story. Eighty-six years ago in the city of Minneapolis, MN, Evelyn Helen Johnson was born on June 29, 1934, at 6:14 pm. It was a very hot summer day, 104°, and Evie's mother, Helen Evelyn, was in labor with no air conditioning. There were fans blowing with a bag of ice in front of them. It was not enough to cool the hot labor room.

Evelyn was a child of the great depression. There was little money and jobs were hard to find. Aunt Alice called Evelyn, "Evalinka." Elof, Evelyn's older brother, called her "Gee Gee" because it was hard to say Evelyn when you're only sixteen months older. Gee Gee was her name all the way through high school.

Evelyn was a salutatorian at Vocational High School in Minneapolis. She ranked second highest in the graduating class of 1952. Evelyn worked at William Seltz Attorney at Law. She rode a city bus to St. Paul and delivered corporate documents, Articles of Incorporation, to the State Capitol.

Growing up, Evelyn lived in the basement of tenement housing. Evelyn said it was dreary doing her homework in the basement, so she sat on the front step. Evelyn was 14 when she started dating Harland Countryman. Harland lived a few blocks away. He would drive by her house with a car full of girls, and there was another boy. One day, Harland drove by and asked if she would like to go with them for a root beer. Root beer was 5¢ and 10¢ back then. Evelyn said "yes" and got in the car. This went on until one day, Evelyn got in the car, and it was only Evelyn and Harland.

Evelyn, age 18, and Harland, 24, married in The Finnish Church on July 11, 1952. Vicki was born 16 months later.

Evelyn was in labor for 24 hours with Vicki. Afterward, the nurse, in a white dress and starched hat, stood in the doorway holding Vicki and said, "Friends, Romans, Countryman."

Vicki weighed 5 pounds when she came home from the hospital and needed to be fed every 2 hours. Mom set an alarm, so I would not miss a feeding. Evelyn went to work at the office of Public Health and Nursing when I was only 6 weeks old.

Laura was born 3 years later. Harley was born 2 years after Laura. All 3 of us were born in November. Even our dog, Teddy, a Boston Terrier, was born in November, November 12. When Laura and Harley were born, we became a family. Laura's baby picture was in consideration for the Gerber Baby. Harley has kept us laughing, smiling, and having fun. Mom and Dad raised good kids.

Mother Dear prayed and put her children in God's hands every day. Mother Dear read her Bible every day, daily devotions. God was very strong in her life. When I lived at home, I never heard Mom say a swear word. Maybe "Oh butterfingers" when she dropped something. Dad called her "E-Slip" because she had a tendency to drop things.

Mother Dear gave her children powerful prayers that worked. I remember one Saturday when Harley went to Costco to pick up Mom's drugs. The line into Costco was wrapped around the building. Mom told Harley to just go to the front of the line and say, "I'm here to pick up some drugs for my mom." Mom said, "I'll pray for you." Harley went to the front of the line and said, "I'm here to pick up some drugs for my mom." A Costco employee said, "Go right in." Prayers work.

"I pray for all my kids, yes. I pray for your cars, your vehicles, your traveling, your job, your schooling, and for the kids, and I pray for my friends. I thank God every day for you. My life is good because of you, kids."

Mother Dear gave us the gift of a great memory, powerful determination, artistic creativity, the love of movies, faith, and she taught us how to pray and give thanks. Evie lived her life with love, grace, and gratitude. Evie liked to do crossword puzzles and loved to read. She wrote book reports at school for 50¢. Evie read every book that was given to her.

Mom taught us to be honest, have a solid, good work ethic, and be resourceful. Mother Dear was our first teacher. I learned from mom, the secret of life is smiles, compliments, and thankfulness. If you can make someone happy, you are happy, too.

Mother Dear loved to knit and watch TV. She knitted my husband, Mark, and me matching dune buggy coats. She knitted hats, booties, sweaters, mittens, and a bunting for her grandchildren. Our children were warm, happy, and loved. People noticed and complimented, saying, "Someone's been knitting." Yes, that's my mom.

When Kami was born, Mom became a great-grandmother. Evie wanted to be called G.G. Evie made beautiful, hand-crafted greeting cards. They were made with love and sent with love. When we saw calligraphy on the envelope in the mailbox, we knew it was from G.G.

Mom and Dad brought our family from lower class to middle class. Thank you! Mom was a secretary for 14 years, an executive secretary for 30 years, and worked at Walgreens, CVS, Walmart, and Herberger's 'till she was 81.

Evie enjoyed buying stuff from QVC, a Home Shopping Network on TV. "It's better to have it and not need it than to need it and not have it." A Countryman's way of life. Ya sure you betcha.

We loved to make Mother Dear laugh. Her quick giggle and good, hearty laugh made us want to laugh, too. It's great to hear Mother Dear laugh with pure enjoyment. Sweet and precious memories. It's comforting to know Evie is just a thought away.

Mom's wisdom: Unless we have bad days, how can we appreciate the good days. Take the good with the bad and have good thoughts. Enjoy this day, see the best in it, and make the most of it.

Mom would praise me on our phone calls. She would say, "Keep up the good work and I love you." Mother Dear always said, "On cloudy days, we need to create our own sunshine. Create our own joy." The last words Mom told me: "Find joy in everything. I love you." Mother Dear wants us to live our lives and be happy and have fun in this life.

Evie's death came naturally. Mother Dear always died on the front lawn in Laura's home movies. At Peace on March 13, 2021. Evie was received into the welcoming arms of a loving Lord. "I get to see Jesus' face for the first time. I have a new home, a wonderful place. I can breathe again."

No sorrow, no night. No sorrow in sight. No worries. No fears. No ailments, no aches, no pains. No crying, no tears in heaven. Just smiles and blue skies where the flowers are in forever bloom. Life is good. God is good. Life is short. The next life is forever.

Let us remember her smiling, her laughing, her talking, her sharing, her caring, and her loving. Lots of love. We thank you and we love you, Mom. We thank you and we love you.

"A life
without love
is a year
without summer."
-Swedish Proverb

*"Talk to yourself like you
would to someone you love"*
- Brené Brown

Journey to Being Childless

By Jackie Donegan

 Jackie Donegan is a Medical Massage Therapist and Personal Trainer. Originally from South Bend, Indiana, her adventurous outlook on life has taken her across the US and parts of Europe. Now taking up the mantle as the local Village Healer, Jackie resides in Cork, Ireland, with her husband, Sean, and their two furbabies.

"When Are You Having Kids?"

One of the most dreaded questions to be asked if choosing to be childless in today's society is, "When are you having kids?" The preceding uncertainty of how the conversation is going to play out can be filled with anxiety, pain, and justifiable defensiveness. This can apply to not just cisgender women and men but anyone with a uterus (or suspected uterus) regardless of their gender identity (e.g. trans men/women and non-binary individuals).

Someone's perceived age can also prompt this question. It can typically span from the late teens to early forties for cisgender women, trans women, and female-presenting non-binary individuals. Interestingly, it can span into the fifties or sixties for cisgender men, trans men, and masculine-presenting non-binary individuals. No matter one's age or gender identity when this question is asked, the burden of answering politely seems to fall onto the recipient, as opposed to the oblivious questioner, who may not see how such a personal and intimate inquiry should not be asked in the first place. How did we get here as a society?

The idea of it being acceptable to basically be asking about another's reproductive sex life is rather ridiculous and intrusive. The question might as well be, "How is sexual intercourse with your partner going?" There could be many reasons as to why someone has not had children yet and why it may be insensitive to ask. Perhaps they are not in a relationship where they want to combine genetic material with the other partner. It could be that they or their partner are physically incapable of having children, with or without assistance. There are those who have suffered a single, or multiple, miscarriages and may have decided to not experience the potential loss again.

Those who have become stepparents might be content with the family size and not want to grow it any further. Different stages in life, jobs, finances, and health can play a factor in these decisions. Then there are those of us who have chosen to not have children, even though we are physically and/or financially capable of doing so. This seems to be the most unacceptable reason and usually leads to some of the most uncomfortable or infuriating conversations. Ones that are aimed to intentionally, or unintentionally, make you "see the light" and "change your mind." The fact remains that some of us may have never felt that primordial urge to become parents or are still just choosing to remain childless. But no matter the reason, there is always a personal journey behind them, and mine is no exception.

Gender Norms and Expectations

Having grown up in a large family of nine, parents included, with three older brothers and three younger brothers, the thought of not having children never really crossed my mind. It goes without saying that the gender norms of the 80s and 90s were girls had baby dolls and all things pink; boys had GI Joes and all things blue.

Girls helped out in the kitchen and with indoor chores; boys helped with the yard work and took out the trash. Dresses and makeup; jeans and dirt. Unfortunately for me, I was fighting those norms from the start; just ask my mother about the Easter Sunday dresses. I did not want to play with all things pink and baby dolls. I did not understand why I was the only one who had to wear a dress. I loved playing in the woods, getting muddy, and pretending I was a superhero helping others. I taught myself martial arts from books and in return taught my brothers.

Sports and academics were what preoccupied most of my childhood. Growing up and having children was the last thing on my mind. I wanted to help people. So, when I learned that there were children in the world without parents, I began to think, when I was older, I would choose the adoption route. There were plenty of children that needed a good home, right? So, this was my mindset through my adolescent and teenage years, up through my early twenties. The desire to have a biological child of my own just was not there.

Let The Reproductive Questions Begin

I was in a steady relationship, and my partner at the time had a child of their own. While I enjoyed being a stepparent, it was agreed there would be no more children. But being in a relationship, and of reproductive age, the questions began coming from family and friends. At first, the responses back from me were basic and expected: "Oh, maybe in the future," or "We have plenty of time." These were seemingly acceptable but were many times followed up with, "Oh, it's great being a stepparent, but you'll want one of your own at least." This comment would especially sting, as I had loved the child as my own and did not feel like I needed to have a biological one.

Fast forward to the relationship ending, being single and a few years older. While still in my twenties and not in a relationship, you would think those baby questions would end. Unfortunately, they just changed to comments like, "Oh, you'll find someone," and "You still have time for kids." With these comments came unnecessary pressures and a stigma that being single and childless makes for an incomplete way of life.

I hate to admit that I bought into these pressures and found myself compromising my own expectations. When my next relationship ended with an unintended pregnancy, which resulted in a miscarriage, it really forced me to look at what I wanted in life, yet again, when it came to children. I leaned more to not having any, but I was still open to being a stepparent. A few years later, I found myself in that role for three young children. Just as before, I treated them as if they were my own and yet still felt no need to have any biologically.

Personal Acceptance & Confidence

As the last relationship ended, I entered into the single life. Now in my early 30s, I decided that I would never again be in a parental role. I realized my life was just as meaningful and fulfilling without children. When the comments began again with, "you'll find someone" and "you still have time for kids," my responses became, "I'm perfectly content being single" and "I don't want any kids."

Usually, they would circle back to repeat their first comments, or add-in, "You say that now, just you wait and see." The amount of times I held back the eye-rolling at these comments were so numerous that it must have saved me from being plagued with permanent vertigo.

After moving from Indiana to Ireland, I quickly realized that the "child questions" were just as part of Irish society as they were back in the USA. My friends and colleagues were able to relate to my own experiences, and some of their journeys were even more painful and complicated. So, when I did meet my now-husband, Sean, one of our first conversations was about children.

He had been a carer for his elderly father for years and never had a desire to have children of his own. He had dealt with many insensitive comments and questions surrounding starting a family and would get the same responses back, verbatim, that I would receive. We had a connection and understanding from the beginning.

We also had the realistic understanding to check in with each other, every now and then, just to make sure we were still on the same page or if a deeper conversation was needed. We discussed if we would regret not having children, missing out on grandchildren, or not leaving a legacy behind after we had passed. We came to the conclusion that being the "cool" aunt and uncle could be our legacy. We would enjoy the childless life and continue to pursue our individual and combined dreams. By supporting each other, we can make our own happiness and spoil our two furbabies along the way.

Responses & Insights

We now face the "When are you having kids?" questions together. Some of our responses are polite, most are sarcastic, and for others, you must appreciate the Irish banter:

"We are the Cool Aunt and Uncle!"

"We enjoy kids, love our nieces and nephews, but just don't want any of our own."

"The world is overpopulated as it is…."

"Two words… Climate. Change," or, "The world is already F***ed."

And my husband's favorite response from the beloved Irish comedian, Tommy Tiernan, "Little Fanta filled f***ers!"

Of course, they would usually circle back with something like:

"You're being selfish not having children." (As if this makes any sense at all! Could it not be argued that it is more "selfish" to have a child simply to fulfill a personal parental desire?)

"You're only saying that because he's/she's saying they don't want kids." (Extremely rude to insinuate that we don't think for ourselves in our marriage or communicate our emotions effectively.)

"You'll regret it." (No, we won't. Our life together now is more real than the imaginary children we could have had.)

"You still have time to change your mind." (Realistically, yes, but our choice is still no.)

Change in Conversation

There should be no shame for a person to choose to be childless. Those with children might find this choice intimidating or find that it forces them to face their own choices they have made in life. Either way, if a blunt question about someone's reproductive sex life is asked, as innocent as society makes it appear to be, then the one asking should be prepared for a blunt response or the possibility of hurting someone.

So perhaps get away from asking these types of questions or making those rebuttal comments. Maybe allow the person to bring it up instead, and, if nothing is mentioned, then leave it alone. Let's work together at changing the conversation around having children. The human species is not going to die out because we do not have enough people reproducing. If anything, we are overpopulated, under-resourced, and facing massive climate changes. So let us get rid of those personally intrusive questions, leave those societal expectations in the past and rejoice in our loved ones living a life they have chosen to live. Perhaps we should just mind our own damn business when it comes to the reproductive sex life of those around us. When the urge to ask, "When are you having kids?" presents itself within, take a deep breath and beat that question back down to where it belongs. There are a million and one other topics to discuss in this big beautiful chaotic world, other than how effective sexual intercourse is with someone's partner.

*"Don't wait around for
other people
to be happy for you.
Any happiness
you get you've got to
make yourself."
- Alice Walker*

The Quietest Baby of All

By Isabella Radtke

Isabella Radtke has been a self-proclaimed book-worm since before she could even read, often memorizing stories to read to dolls and family members. Soon to begin in high school, Isabella has continued to persevere and perspire, and continues to study hard, read harder, write the hardest.

We've been waiting for oh so long
Waiting, watching my bump grow
Bellies huge, growing larger
Nine months later I'm 'bout to pop
Waiting, watching for someone
Never knowing that we would
Be getting
Be getting
The quietest baby of all

Finally, I say enough
Take me to the hospital
Waiting, watching doctors run
Is something wrong with my bump?
Nothing's wrong she says to me
Lying, lying through her teeth
I ask you when the baby comes

She answers, soon, my darling soon
Now I know, looking back
That she knew just what I got
What I got, what I got
The quietest baby of all

Into labor
Oh the pain
Shouting screaming
Oh, not nice
Why must I pay such a price
I'll do it again, and again and again
I'd do it all over again
If only I had not gotten
The quietest baby of all

Finally, the pain has stopped
The baby's out, he's out fin'lly
The doctors run
The nurses hurry
Why can't i please hold my baby?
Then suddenly, it all stops
No more running, no more clocks
Time is ticking, they check their watches
Slowly moving, not much rushing
I ask again to hold my baby
I want to rest my eyes on him
He or her or something else
I'll love them all the same
Black or white, latino or
Any other color
I want my baby

Finally, she hands me him

He's not crying or moving
She says she's sorry
There's nothing at all
That she could have ever done
The baby was doomed from the start
He will never run or walk
He will never ever talk
My house will never have him running
Down the long and empty halls
My house will never hear his chatter
Because he is
The quietest baby of all
The quietest baby of all
The quietest, stillest, deadest baby
Of all

*"We come in many
different shapes and sizes,
and we need to support each other
and our differences.*

*Our beauty
is in our differences."*
- Carré Otis

The Dress

By Carol Griffith

 Carol Griffith is an artist with a background in watercolor painting and photography. A modern renaissance woman, Carol has stories and tales from her previous lives in a variety of creative outlets. Today, she paints mostly ladies – her friends – in a humorous fashion when she is not taking photographs of local scenery and events.

"Where did you get that dress?" asked Sharon.

"Hey, that was a great dress. I looked really hot in that dress," said Dixie. "I wore it to a gala in Kentucky when we lived there. Dom wore a tux. It was a really great party."

"Purple polyester, hum," said Carol.

"With purple sequins – don't forget the sequins," said Sharon.

"Oh, I love all the tucks and folds in the bodice. That must have added a few inches to your already ample bust. Woo, woo," said Carol.

"I think I'll try it on," said Chris.

"Listen you guys, don't make fun of that dress. Dixie was really hot when she wore it, " said Dom. "She really turned me on."

"Hell, Dom, everything turns you on," said Carol.

"I wore spiky silver sandals and rhinestone jewelry," said Dixie. "Wait, I have an album with photos from that party. Hey, Dom, see if you can find the album from 1980."

"Oh my God, look at the white eyeshadow," said Carol.

"And look at her hairdo," said Sharon.

"You're right, Dixie! You really were a sex goddess."

"Okay, you guys, what do you think?" asked Chris. "Am I hot?"

"Oh, it is even better on," said Carol. "I'll bet if you twirl, the little points on the hem will flare out."

"Geeze, Chris, stop it! You're showing your underpants! Hey, Dom, you want to see Chris' underpants?"

"I'm going to wet my underpants if I don't stop laughing," said Carol.

"Look how many cars are stopping! Keep twirling, Chris!"

"You ladies sure know how to put on a garage sale," said a smiling customer. "By the way, how much is that purple dress?"

"Don't even think about it, Harry!" said his wife.

Turmoils of Loving Forever

By Isabella Radtke

 Isabella Radtke has been a self-proclaimed book-worm since before she could even read, often memorizing stories to read to dolls and family members. Soon to begin in high school, Isabella has continued to persevere and perspire, and continues to study hard, read harder, write the hardest.

"Painting is a metaphor for control. Every choice is mine- the canvas, the color, the brush. As a child I had little sense of the world, nor my place in it, but art taught me that one's vision can be achieved with sheer force of will. The same is true of life, provide one refuses to let anything stand in one's way." - Niklaus 'Klaus' Mikaelson

This is that moment. The one you wish never to happen. The thought that keeps you up at night, staring at your ceiling. The moment that is secretly there, like a heavy, iron cloud of despair laying overhead - no matter how happy you are in the best time of your life, it is still all you can think about regardless. It's the prayer you beg of, from whatever Gods are up there- the many offerings you make to them, willing all your worldly possessions if only this time doesn't ever exist, this doesn't happen, it's safely avoided forever. It's the bargains you make up in your head, the monster under your bed, and the Masters whip coming out on your bareback in front of your family's eyes.

111

This is the thing that you think of in your mind when you are alone, thinking what you will say if it does happen, planning what your response will be and what you will do first if it does come. You hope and pray and wish upon your shooting star, every day and night and every time you take a breath, knowing just how real the possibilities are. Only to find, your prayers have all gone unanswered. Your bargains were not sufficient. Your pleas were not loud enough to be heard. Your offerings were not worthy. And in that moment you planned so much for, you find that your thoughts are blank, you cannot function, and you know for real, that the world is a very cold, dark place because the one thing, the one person, the one goal that made it all worth it, that kept you going in your darkest times and helped you rise from your straw pallet in your cabin.... is gone forever.

He's here. He isn't supposed to be here, not yet. I'm supposed to see him in two weeks, when my brother and Poppa and my fiancé are returned to me at last, after such a long time away from me, because Momma invited him over for a party to celebrate.

He isn't supposed to be here.

He isn't supposed to be here.

He isn't supposed to be here.

That's all that runs through my brain. That's all that I can think of right now. I only stand here, looking out of my window in the sitting room, as he slowly approaches me, his head bowed low, shoulders stooped, as if he's aged a thousand years in the three months I have not seen him. He looks up, meets my eyes, and that's when I know that I really have lost someone I love, and he's not coming back again.

He finally reaches the big door; I almost don't hear his knocks over my blood, now pounding in my ears faster every moment that he stands. My momma enters the sitting room, still in her night clothes. She rubs her eyes of sleep then looks out the window, next to me.

"Open the door, Rachel," she says. Her voice is unlike any I have ever heard her speak before, soft and raspy; it's nothing like the sweet, smooth voice that carries her stories high and low as it swoops you along with it. She hangs on the fireplace, looking as weak as I feel, though I cannot show it right now. She looks nothing like the tall figure that has always carried herself with pride and power in the past, no matter how little we had.

"Open the door. Let him in," she repeats. I stand where I am, not moving, not taking my eyes off of him. I silently try to will him to walk away, to leave me be, and I try to imagine this moment isn't happening. My thoughts are running faster and more wild than two tomcats trapped in a bag together.

I see my little brother, Aaron, the day he won the biggest race on our plantation; his small face was seeped in sweat and dirt, tongue slightly poking out of his mouth, as he charged to the front of the group, whole body tense as he flew down the fields to the finish line at last. Then, I see our poppa, his face merry and his eyes crinkling at the corners as he laughs at my aunts retelling of their childhood fun. I see my future husband that I am to marry this year, as he lays on his back in the middle of the cotton field, after curfew, watching the star- the picture of pure and peace.

"My star. Right there. It never moves, never, every night, and I can always count on it to be there for me and to watch over me, day and night. They call it the North Star, but I've always called it my Love Star. I want to be there for you, I want to be your star, Rachel. Please? Marry me, and we can be together and only have to rely on each other for guidance."

Of course I said yes.

My mother tries to push past me to get the door, but I hold her back with a strength that surprises us both.

"I will," I whisper.

She nods, then slumps against the wall. We both know what he will tell us, both are bracing ourselves for the whip to swing, the ax to drop, for our lives to shatter. I hold on to these precious moments before I open the door. The 'before', the time we have until we find out. Regardless of who has been sold away. And yes, I know they have been sold, because all these men had been happy here with us and would not leave me or my mother or my sister alone, ever.

"Who?" is all I ask.

Screw grammar, screw greetings, and screw manners. I don't care. I only wish to know, *need* to know, and I need to know now. Before I lose my grip on the small bit of sanity I have left without Petter here. Before I break. Before I slam the door shut on his face and run to my pallet and pretend that he isn't here, like I hadn't heard him knocking today at all.

"Rachel…"

"W-who?" I stammer again, interrupting him. Now. Tell me now. Who is it? Who has left me forever?

I probably will have to ask Momma's permission. Only, I know what she will say, and I also know that it won't be what I need to hear from her. The only other alternative would be to ask Poppa, but if I get caught by overseer's in the tobacco fields, where I am not to be, we will both be punished even more. Anyways, he won't give me the answer I need either. I need one of them to say yes because it is required to always get your parents blessing when being married on this plantation. And if I don't get a blessing, the marriage won't be legal or considered to have even happened here in the southern colonies.

"Just ask," Petter hisses to me. "You won't know unless you do, and there is a chance she will say yes. If you don't ask at all, there's no way she can say yes to begin with!" I don't tell him that he doesn't know what it feels like because Petter knows as well as I that he doesn't. Petter got sold away from his family nearly seven years ago, so he doesn't need their permission; however, the pain of not knowing anything about my own family is something I do not envy of Petter.

I catch the plates my future husband almost drops and breaks because Mistress will hear the sound and kick us both out of the kitchen, and the kitchen is the only place Petter and I might talk in private.

"Give those to me right fast, before you get us discovered!" I snap at him.

Petter pauses then turns around fully to look me in my eyes. He stands just a few inches taller than me, but now it feels like a mighty horse looking down upon a tiny gnat. He places the plates on the counter- too quickly and they almost slide off, but he catches them in time, making me wince for him. He looks at me again and takes my delicate face between his huge hands.

"Rachel. I promised you forever. Did I not?" he asks slowly. I am instantly taken back to the night he took me out to his place under the stars in the tobacco field. That was the first time any man had ever told me he loved me and wanted to be there for me "forever and always" and to "never let you go, no matter what may come between us." I get a shiver of excitement, right here in the kitchen, even all these weeks later.

"Yes, you did, Petter," I whisper back to him. Petter opens his mouth again to speak more words to me, but then we hear shrieking.

"RACHEL! OH, RACHEL! *DO* COME QUICK!" Mistress hollers, loud as anything else in the world. Petter and I both start, but Petter still holds my face. He glances to the window in the kitchen, meant to let out warm breezes so that pies that I make, along with the other kitchen hands, may set out to cool after being in the oven. Petter releases my face, and the instant he does, I long for his touch once more. Inside Petter's hands, there is no Mistress. There are no floggings, or work, or shrieks. There is only he and I.

But if I do not let Petter go, we will both be in great, great deals of trouble. I must go help Mistress. She has probably found a mouse under her chair once more - never mind that I am as terrified by rats and mice as she is; if Mistress wishes me to do something, then I must do it immediately. I do not think she knows, nor cares, how many mice and rats are in my cabin. In my bed, crawling on my plate sometimes, occasionally even *inside* of it, as Momma sometimes cooks rats at night. Momma is always cautious so that Master and Mistress cannot see the flames of the fire she makes. I hate the rats worst of all; they are bigger and have no fear- the mice run and scare off instead of trying to bite my ankles.

Later, I go out to the fields to take the plantation workers a pail of water to drink. Most all are men and boys; women work mostly in the kitchens to earn their keep and take care of Mistress. I feel the pail of water banging against my legs as I walk- BANG, BANG, BANG it goes as I trek up to the tobacco fields that Master has growing. The pail announces my arrival, so I don't have to holler out. Aaron tends to make fun of me quite a bit because of the noise, no matter that honestly he is louder. Seven is a wild age for boys and a tiring time for their older sisters. Poppa will scold him for picking fun at me, but there is not much else he can do. The other men and boys in the fields also tease me, and Poppa cannot fend them all off, or else the overseers will think him to be trouble and a disturbance.

The men are sweating so furiously, I am able to smell their stench from afar. I wish I could just hand them the pail so that they may drink it themselves, but I have seen one girl, younger than I, do this before. Mistress saw, as did the overseers, and no one has seen the girl since; we all believe that she has been sold away. Her mother knows not where she is and is in great distress for her child.

The men are now approaching me, some catcalling and picking on me for my noise. I ignore them, as Momma has always taught me to do.

"Where is my poppa, please?" I ask one of the men; I think he is called Henri.

"Girl, give me my drink!" Henri demands angrily. "I been working all day and you refuse to give me a drop!"

I imagine in my head putting the pail behind my back and insisting that he tell me, but I don't. Instead, I take the dipper from the pail and offer it to Henri's mouth to drink.

"Little girl, that's my turn!"

"Give me a drink!"

"How comes he gets more than I?"

Many are angry at me, but I know better than to respond to any calls. They are exhausted and have no better people to take out their frustrations on, and so they target me, Momma says. I am to ignore them and let their insults roll off of my back as if nothing has been said.

"Do you know where my poppa is?" I try again when I offer the next person the water dipper. It is a small boy; he can't be more than eight or nine winters old.

"Harry, right?" I guess his name.

"No," he mutters. "Give it to me." I give his water.

As the line goes on, I become more panicked. I try to stay calm, but the more men go down the line and the more men who are not my poppa, I grow more anxious. Why would he not be here? Has an overseer taken him to talk? Has he been forbidden water today for not picking enough leeches off of the tobacco leaves in time, or for missing too many in a row? I beg the men for my poppa, but they know not of his whereabouts, nor do they care. They only wish for their water, not to be pestered during their only break.

I realize that Aaron and Petter have also not been in line, and at the same moment that this thought crosses my mind and I begin to really panic, I hear shouts coming from the horses barn.

117

Aaron! He must be in there, the foolish, foolish child. He loves the horses as much as his own life. I hope no one has found him, but from the shouting and rising noises, I know that they have.

"Master!" I cry. "Master, he means no harm, please!"

I drop the pail of water and throw myself down the hill to the barn. I can only imagine what Master is thinking right now- that Aaron had plans to steal one of his horses and run away to freedom, or that Aaron might be a thief, hiding in the barn until no one was watching and then take all of the horses back to his own farm.

"Rachel?" Aaron's quiet voice says my name. He sounds baffled to hear me; he must have lost track of time, the forgetful dreamer.

"Aaron, you had me worried out of my wits! Who was that shouting just now?" I ask frantically, taking his tiny face between my hands and searching his body for marks or signs of bleeding.

"Oh. I was just startled. Penny Chance backed up when I had my back turned, and I tripped. I'm fine, I promise." Aaron shrugs. I know I am not to hit hit and that Aaron is seven so he does not think as fast and as smart as I do, but I do wish to grab his tiny, bone-skinny shoulders and shake him well sometimes.

"Aaron, you frightened me," I scold, quieting myself down and calming my racing heart. Sometimes I remind myself too much of Momma. I shake my head at him then turn to leave. I will see Aaron again tonight, in our cabin together, and maybe I will ask my family's blessing. I ponder this and how to propose the question to Momma on my way back up the hill to pick up the water pail and go back to Mistress. Laundry time now, and she will take a nap as I do. In all this commotion with Aaron, I'd completely forgotten about Poppa and Petter being missing. I will find out soon, and when I do, there will be no shaking heads in annoyance, only shaking of shoulders in tears and sobbing.

Returning to my cabin, only Petter's and my engagement is on my mind. When I walk in the modest home, I have to duck my head to enter because the ceiling is so stooped. Master has no time, no patience nor kindness inside his heart to give his slaves better living quarters, but at least we have a cabin. When Momma was first sold to this plantation, she says that all slaves slept outside, in the middle of the tobacco fields, even when it was raining and storming. I shudder to think- thunder scares me, something fierce, always has.

As soon as I get in the cabin, Momma throws her arms around me, sobbing. Now, mind, my Momma is the strongest woman ever. She helps others before herself and has stood through leaving her family when she was only fourteen years old. I could never do that! Momma has never, ever, ever cried. EVER. Her whole body was shaking with huge sobs, wracking through her body as she held me to her chest. I admit I could not think, so I merely stood there with my momma draped across my body.

"I thought they took you, too," she whispered softly into my ear. "I thought I'd never see you again."

"Who did they take?" I demanded, shoving her off of me with more strength than I'd meant.

"We can't know until tomorrow morn. You know as well as I, your poppa is as strong headed and thick skulled as a mule pulling a heavy cart to work." This is true- Master and the overseers have often nights kept poppa behind to 'have a word' with him. Momma says he's strong headed. Poppa says he's overly opinionated. Master says he's a rebel who needs an eye. I say he's stubborn, like me.

"What about..." my voice trails off as I search the cabin for my little brother. Momma has her eyes shining with tears again.

"Rachel..." she whispers thickly. "I am so sorry, baby."

I've never noticed how dark the night could be. It is swelling around me, pitch black and dead silent, save my sobs. I run from home, tearing through the night and plunging myself into the sticky heat and humidity that came with living here.

He's gone... he's gone...

Aaron's gone. I'll never see him again, and it's all my fault.

Finally, my legs can take me no further. I have never been so incredibly exhausted in this way before, never felt this empty and alone. The loneliness sinks in, quite suddenly. I have nowhere to go but back to the plantation, where Aaron is not.

"I…want… I want my brother!" I scream. I don't care if the overseers hear me. I don't care if I frighten Mistress in her sleep. Their threats cannot pierce my heart as harshly as Aaron and Petter and Poppa have, and now they cannot hurt me anymore. I have been thrust into a dull blade, and it tears my insides apart. I try to put my hands across my mouth, but they do nothing to muffle my heart as it throbs in my chest. Why do I live, stay, breathe here while they are all sent away.

I scream again, emptying my chest and my lungs into the black space around me. It threatens to drown me, so I scream louder. I scream and scream and scream, until there is nothing left inside of me to scream anymore.

My knees hit the ground. The tobacco stalks are digging into my legs, but I feel them not. Bugs crawl over my legs, but I notice them not. Thunder rumbles in the distance, but I tremble not. Not in fear, not anymore. My greatest fear has come true, and there is no stopping that anymore. I am completely, utterly and totally powerless in all ways possible because the only three people that I have lived for, fought for, stood up for and stayed up all night for… are gone.

Three weeks later

A knock on the Mistress' door. Momma looks up from where she stands by the fireplace but doesn't move more than a half-glance up from prodding the logs in the fireplace. She has been like this ever since we found out- silent, a quiet shadow of the powerful woman she once was with Poppa by her side.

"Please open the door, Rachel." Mistress asks me.

I nod quietly and rise from my chair by the fire. I heave the heavy, ornate wooden door opened, straining to pull it wide enough. I freeze. I recognize the man at the door immediately- how could I not?

Every slave on every plantation knows who their auctioneer is. It is the unspoken rule among us, much like the saying "keep your friends close, keep your enemies closer." It is the slave auctioneer for our town. Tall as my poppa, skinny as the sugar cane drawings I see sometimes in the Masters working room, with hair as white as a Percheron horse's coat yet as thin as straw.

Our slave auctioneer has no taste and no color about him, so pale and white is he. He is nothing but cold and heartless, such as all white men. After Petter had left, I had not realized how much I would miss his smile across his face, his laugh sounding much like a donkey that could not breathe right. The world is a cold, cold place, and the white men are even colder.

The slave auctioneer clears his throat loudly in front of me, and I realize I have been standing in front of him like a ninny and not letting him in. He isn't supposed to be here, not yet. I'm supposed to see him in two weeks, when my brother and Poppa and my fiancé are returned to me. That's what my mistress informed me when I asked her about my family's whereabouts, and why. Apparently, Petter and Aaron had not been working efficiently in the fields, and Poppa was taken because he was influencing Aaron and slowing him down.

He isn't supposed to be here.

He isn't supposed to be here.

He isn't supposed to be here.

That's all that runs through my brain. That's all that I can think of right now. I only stand here, looking out of my window in the sitting room, as he slowly approaches me, his head bowed low, shoulders stooped, as if he's aged a thousand years in the three months I have not seen him. He looks up, meets my eyes, and that's when I know that I really have lost someone I love, and he's not coming back again.

121

My blood is pounding in my ears, that's all I hear. I almost don't hear him clearing his throat once more. Mistress asks me to meet her in the kitchen momentarily and leaves. My momma looks over my shoulder, not moving from her position but still able to tell who it is.

"Let him in the door, Rachel," she says. Her voice is unlike any I have ever heard her speak before, soft and raspy, nothing like the sweet, smooth voice that carries her stories high and low and swoops you along with it.

"Open the door wider. Let him in," she repeats, her voice taking an unnatural edge to it I have never heard her use before. I stand where I am, not moving, not taking my eyes off of him. I silently will him to walk away, leave me be, pretend this moment isn't happening, though my thoughts are running wildly.

My mother tries to push past me to get the door, but I hold her back with a strength that surprises us both.

"I will," I croak out. She nods, then slumps against the wall. We both know what he will tell us; both are bracing ourselves for the whip to swing, the ax to drop, for our lives to shatter. I hold onto these precious moments before I open the door. The before, the time we have until we find out. Regardless of who will be taken, all these men had been happy here with us and would not leave me or my mother or my sister alone. But they don't have a choice.

"Who?" is all I ask.

Screw grammar, screw greetings, and screw manners. I don't care. I only wish to know, need to know, and I need to know now. Before I lose my grip. Before I break. Before I slam the door shut on his face and run to my pallet and pretend that he isn't here, like I hadn't heard him knocking today.

"Child-"

"Who?" I repeat, interrupting him. "Now. Tell me now. Who has left me forever?"

"It was Petter. Petter and your father," the Slave Auctioneer mumbles, as though he is ashamed of what he has done in selling them away from me.

"Why?" I demand. I'm being more rude than I have ever been in my life, and this is not how Momma raised me to be. He doesn't seem to notice my anger. I'm justified, I know- Petter would never hurt a fly, and my poppa is even more so in this way.

"Petter had run from the fields into town. Your poppa was keeping guard outside the silversmith's shop for him while Petter stole an item of great value. The police were called, and they were both arrested for thievery and running away from their Master and for going into town without permission." The slave auctioneer pauses, and finally, he looks up to meet my eyes.

I know the item that Petter had stolen. It cannot be anything else. Only Petter would have the audacity and the bravery to do such a thing. I ask anyway because I *want* Momma to hear his words as much as I *need* to hear them.

"What- what was it that he stole, please?" The auctioneer looked me dead into my eyes for the first time.

"A ring, miss. He attempted to steal a ring." His voice is no longer soft and shaky like it was before, now full of power and anger and steel. His eyes flame and everything about his posture speaks his anger louder than words.

I nod silently. Tears streamed down my face, but I couldn't care less. I should be ashamed to be seen in such a state by an adult, but I find that I am not.

"Thank you." I whisper. Then I close the door in his face and go back to my seat by the fireplace.

##

"Miss Rachel! Miss Rachel!" a voice hollers out to me. I straighten up from the flower garden I am taming for Mistress as she is too old to do so herself anymore.

I call back, "What is it?"

"It's a box! For you!" the squeaky voice yells in elation.

"A box? What is in it?" I ask.

"Open it, open it!"

I laugh to myself at the joy that fills this child's entire being as she hurdles her way to me. She shoves the box in my hands- it is miniscule enough to fit inside my palm, which surprises me. It is black and has fuzz around it.

"He told me not to tell you who it was from, so don't ask me," the child says stubbornly, raising her head high and sticking her nose in the air.

I laugh again then open it slowly at her begging. What is inside it? I have almost never gotten any mail or any present before in my life, and at this, a thrill runs through my veins.

It is small, indeed. Small and has a band as black as ebony, black as the night my lover was taken from me. It is set in a cushion, silver as the stars and by far the most sparkly thing I have ever seen. The stone that rests atop the night- black band is what really catches my attention. Huge and polished to a shine brighter than the sun in midday summer, smoothed and sanded down to fine, precise edges that are all pointed and firm. The ring is the most beautiful thing in the entire world to me.

I know it is from Petter- he works in a mine now, so he would have found it himself. He would have put it in his pocket or his satchel. He would have stayed up all night to sand it just right, polish it to the shiniest glint, and make sure it was the biggest and best for me.

I know in my heart, we will probably never see each other again. I also know this realization will not change in the near future, much as I may daydream about it. And I also know that, no matter how far we are apart, if Petter can find a way to smuggle a diamond ring all the way from his mines to my plantation without it going astray or breaking... he still loves me. He will always love me, and I him. We may be billions of miles apart, may never see the other's face again, but we will be bonded through the chains of marriage. Maybe not legally, as I never spoke to Momma about it; when she tries to bring it up, I turn her down. But we are married through our love, and that is all that matters to me.

"Wait child, before you go... could you send a letter to the mail carriage before it leaves?" I hurry to sneak a piece of parchment and a quill and ink. I scratch out just two words onto it, so that Mistress will not notice. I haven't much time, and my words are not clean and neat. My hands are shaking terribly bad, but I need to get this down fast, before the mail carriage goes away, and I cannot send mail again for another many months.

There are so many words I wish to tell him, to ask him how he is, to tell him about the plantation... but in the end, there are only two words he needs to read, two words he wants me to write most of them all.

"I DO"

And then I ask Mistress, without even looking over my shoulder to her, for something that I have never asked for my entire life, having used only mud and crushed berries before in the past. I ask her for paints.

Reds as bright as fire and as robust as blood, greens that could compete with what I imagine the garden of Eden to look like, and blues as Petter's eyes. Perfect. I work tirelessly through the nights and early in the mornings. I put my heartbreak and all of my pain into the painting. The paints have been thrown onto the grounds where Petter took me first and declared his eternal love for me. I had put a tarp I made myself over the painting, to protect it from the rain, but I know it will not do much in the future. The animals will come, the grass will grow over, the rain will get through, the winds will pull the tarp off. But maybe that's the point. Everything good must come to an end.

When I finally declare the painting finished, it is my mother who finds me first. When she sees the finished product, she tears up instantly. I don't need to look at her to know. I am still numb sometimes, but the painting draws the pain away and distracts me enough to push the pain and the passion away. I take my emotions and throw them into my art.

I think back, to when a foreign visitor had come to see Master and discuss slaves at auction. I don't remember him well, but one thing I do remember is something he said when he first saw some of Petter's paintings and little drawings and sketches. Now, standing here and looking down on my masterpiece, I can hear his deep, raspy voice. I can hear his foreign accent, British I find out later from the other older slave women, and what he said to Petter when he thought no one else was around to hear:

"Painting is a metaphor for control. Every choice is yours- the canvas, the color, the brush. As a child I had little sense of the world, nor my place in it, like you, but art taught me that one's vision can be achieved with sheer force of will, little one. The same is true of life, provide one refuses to let anything stand in one's way."

I didn't understand the meaning of this, and Petter refused to explain it to me ever, insisting instead that I would know it in my own terms, when I was ready to understand. I wish I could tell him that I understand now. I wish I could show him this. I wish I could see him again. I wish, I wish, I wish.

I know he would be proud at his depiction, and he would be pleased to see the white dress I wear, and the illogical red carpet at our feet as I walk down the rows of tobacco fields to meet him at our own altar to be married.

And whenever I am feeling down on my luck, whenever I need someone warm to hold, I know my poppa is working hard to earn his freedom to then come here and free me. When Master is hollering his worst, whenever I am in trouble, I remember Aaron and how he was always rebelling in crazy ways I cannot even begin to imagine how he pulled off. And most of all, when there are stars in the sky, I watch them and think about how Petter is watching the same stars that I am. They are always there for me no matter what is going on in my life, and Poppa wraps me up in his arms. You can find bits of joy in the middle of a storm if you just look for it; that is what, I have found, throughout this struggle. There is no storm too strong to take away love, and I will see them all someday.

"Be strong,
be fearless,
be beautiful.
And believe that
anything is possible
when you have the
right people there to
support you."
- Misty Copeland

Awards

First Place

"The Birth of My Freshman Year"
by Barb Conlin

Second Place

"Limber as a Rag"
by Angie Klink

Third Place

"Pivotal Pages"
by Patricia Rossi

Congratulations to this year's winners. Gal's Guide Library is honored to share the stories of all of our authors with the world. We offered a space, but the voices are their own.

2022 Judges were: Katie Harris (President of Gal's Guide), Bonnie Fillenwarth (Vice President of Gal's Guide), Lindsey Taylor (Owner of Four-Eyed Media), Elyssa Everling (Johnson County Librarian), and Dr. Leah Leach (Executive Director of Gal's Guide).

About Gal's Guide

Gal's Guide to the Galaxy is a 501(c)3 nonprofit that provides multimedia education about women's history. We have podcasts, school programs, outreach events, workshops, book clubs, and more.

The Gal's Guide Library is the hub of the organization and the first women's history lending library in the United States. Library cards are free. Borrowing books is free. All of our books for lending are written by women or about women. The Gal's Guide Library specializes in biographies, memoirs, and autobiographies.

The Mission

Gal's Guide's mission is to provide an independent women's history library to preserve, collect, share and champion women's achievements and lessons learned. We will act as a catalyst to creators who utilize our resources to guide others to these amazing role models who have been waiting in the shadows of history for too long.

The Gal's Guide Library is located in the Nickel Plate Arts Campus
107 S. 8th Street
Noblesville, Indiana 46060

We accept book donations of all kinds.
We accept financial donations of all kinds.

To learn more visit www.galsguide.org

Made in the USA
Coppell, TX
16 April 2022

76622453R00080